Unless otherwise noted all Scripture quotations are taken from THE HOLY BIBLE, NEW INTERNATIONAL VERSION®, NIV® Copyright © 1973, 1978, 1984, 2011 by Biblica, Inc.® Used by permission. All rights reserved worldwide.

Scripture quotations marked (NLT) are taken from the Holy Bible, New Living Translation, copyright © 1996, 2004, 2007 by Tyndale House Foundation. Used by permission of Tyndale House Publishers, Inc., Carol Stream, Illinois 60188. All rights reserved.

Scripture taken from the New King James Version® (NKJV). Copyright © 1982 by Thomas Nelson, Inc. Used by permission. All rights reserved."

The ESV® Bible (The Holy Bible, English Standard Version®) copyright © 2001 by Crossway, a publishing ministry of Good News Publishers. ESV® Text Edition: 2011. The ESV® text has been reproduced in cooperation with and by permission of Good News Publishers. Unauthorized reproduction of this publication is prohibited. All rights reserved.

Scripture taken from the NEW AMERICAN STANDARD BIBLE®, Copyright © 1960,1962,1963,1968,1971,1972,1973,1975,1977,1995 by The Lockman Foundation. Used by permission.

Scripture taken from the Revised Standard Version of the Bible (RSV), copyright © 1946, 1952, and 1971 the Division of Christian Education of the National Council of the Churches of Christ in the United States of America. Used by permission. All rights reserved.

Acknowledgments

I want to thank my husband, Bill, and my three children, Carrie Anne, Jacob and Noah, for their steadfast support and love and for allowing me to use memories of our life together to enrich my writings. I also want to thank my friend Amy Concannon not only for her encouragement to write, but also for her final read-through before publication.

In addition I wish to thank **Bible Gateway** as a most helpful resource in locating parallel Scriptures in a convenient and timely manner.

"Restore to me the joy of your salvation…" Psalm 51:12

Contents

1. Doors — 1
2. Doors Part Two — 5
3. I'm Losing It! — 9
4. Lessons from Maude — 11
5. I Can Do This! — 13
6. Whose Idea Was This Anyway? — 17
7. I Can… But Should I? — 21
8. But You're So Good At It! — 23
9. You Know How I Feel — 27
10. No, But I Could Have — 29
11. Lessons from Jim — 33
12. Listening to Voices — 35
13. Don't Waste My Time! — 39
14. No, I Really Can't — 43
15. I Didn't Really Mean It! — 47
16. A Trio of Saints — 51
17. If I Can, Why Can't You? — 55
18. What Do You Want from Me? — 59
19. Coals of Kindness — 63
20. Who Died and Left You in Charge? — 67
21. Can I Help You? — 71
22. Left Behind — 75
23. Remote Access — 79
24. It's in the Bag! — 81
25. You'll Get Used to It! — 85

26. You're Not the Boss of Me!	89
27. Pity Pots	93
28. Listening for the Applause	95
29. Runoff	99
30. Lessons from Milton	103
31. There's a Word for It	107
32. Tacking	111
33. I Need a Job!	115
34. How Do I Love Thee?	119
35. Now What?	123
36. Pace Yourself!	127
37. Falling	131
38. I Don't Know My Own Strength!	135
39. It Must Be Nice	139
40. You Make Me Feel So Young	143
41. Making Time For…	147
42. No Questions Asked	151
43. Swerving	155
44. None of Your Beeswax!	159
45. Thanks	163
46. It All Blends Together	167
47. Watching (An Advent Conversation)	171
48. This Can't Wait! (A Christmas Conversation)	175
49. The Gift of Giving (A Christmas Conversation)	179
50. What Did You Expect? (A Christmas and New Year Conversation)	183

Preface

Throughout my life, people and situations I like to call "joy suckers" have tried to limit my full appreciation of the experiences God has gifted to me. I have discovered and am still discovering how to keep those negative influences in check.

When we cannot in any way measure up to the yardstick we or others put next to our lives, the only answer is to continually seek the Lord's forgiveness and remind ourselves to drop our guilt at the cross. My hope is that though my various writings you will feel the acceptance of our less-than-perfect understanding of what being a Christian involves.

The conversation begins….

Doors

The doors of our lives come in all shapes and sizes. Some small doors open to amazing futures, while what we think are important doors reveal only disappointments.

Life changes… and doors close behind us. They can be locked, barred, and sealed. Yet we pound against them in panic or grief, willing the return of the time and place on the other side.

Sometimes we see a door closing and greet the news with relief. Thank goodness that's over! Other closing doors breathe a quiet whisper of regret.

Several years ago my life began a series of door openings and closings. At the time, my teaching career was humming along and the music ministry at church was in full swing. My children were past the college years, and my husband and I could take a momentary sigh of contentment. Little did I expect what doors the Lord was starting to move.

My friend Amy, who is my personal guide to current literature, sat across from me in a coffee shop near our favorite haunt… the local bookstore. The "How is everything?" that usually gets the "Fine" response, this time brought tears into her eyes. Life was good, but she felt disconnected… from her Lord.

Now this wasn't a faith issue. No, this was something different. She talked about needing a time with other women to look into scriptures and topics… without homework or feeling the guilt when she couldn't always make the "class." We talked about the women at church who had careers outside the home and often taught Sunday School, two things that kept them from attending some of the Bible studies. These women didn't need more on their plates to do; they needed a time and place to just "land" spiritually. I realized we were talking about me too.

We began to lay out a plan for a once-a-month Saturday morning "no guilt" encounter for women. That plan became a reality within a few weeks. Now I really didn't need one more thing on my plate, but I felt this was something I could do, without compromising my other responsibilities... too much. I would take the "no guilt" part of this to heart and not let it consume me. I could hear a door opening.

Then the one door I didn't expect to move, at least for another five years, began to close. My husband was the one who sensed it coming and encouraged me to make the most of my time. That last year of full-time teaching was filled with every creative project I had ever put off for the "next year." The teacher-in-the-classroom door firmly closed, yet I didn't let it hit me in the back.

After that abrupt end-of-my-career experience, there were some new doors I thought I was going to open, but they wouldn't budge. I even had the right key (abilities, talents, gifts) and the handle turned. But nothing happened.

Those early months of trial and error actually became a gift... a time to become more aware of which doors were desirable or even possible. And I tried not to stubbornly keep knocking on those that wouldn't open. I began to see that doors that *did* open were the ones that led me on a closer walk with my Lord.

I finally said yes to speaking at a one-day women's retreat. That first retreat turned into seven, and I was able to help my Christian sisters grow stronger in their faith walk. The monthly "no guilt" encounters continued for another six years before it was time to close that door. And during those years I developed a series of ongoing reflections that I emailed to my group of "Sisters Who Are Busy." Those reflections turned into a three-year series of blogs. And surprise! Some of my most faithful readers were men!

Those were the doors that seemed to be swinging wide open with just a gentle push from me and a warm welcome from the Lord.

But now it's time to move on to another arena, another audience. Those words that so many have told me speak to their hearts… those three years of conversations with my readers and my Lord… many are now contained in this first book.

I am boldly going through this new door and can't wait to see what's on the other side!

Doors Part Two

It had been a cold, rainy week, the week before Christmas 2010. The streets were still wet from the most recent Southern California downpour, but we had no plans for that evening. Just a quiet time with our three children.

And then the doorbell rang. I'm usually the one who answers the door when we aren't expecting anyone in particular, since my husband doesn't like to deal with the random person on our front porch.

Well, there was Santa! I unlocked the security screen door and welcomed him in. Really? Did I just open my home up to a random Santa? But then I heard his voice and caught the twinkle in his eye. It was my neighbor from two doors up the street.

"It's *Santa*, Dear!" was my reassurance to my husband, who gave me a wide-eyed look as if I had just invited in, at best, a lunatic and, at worst, a serial killer. I must say I enjoyed his uneasiness.

—⁂—

It was a cold, rainy evening the night I launched my blog site... three weeks later. My daughter and I were making the final decisions and putting together the site's "best to date" look. This was the culmination of two weeks of writing, searching, consulting with friends, etc. It was time to let others in. Time to click the final OK.

Almost immediately I started getting feedback, reassurances from friends that this was a good thing. The speed of sharing took my breath away. My daughter was beside herself with excitement for me.

But within a few minutes a mild panic set in. What if I couldn't meet the expectations of what these people were looking for? What if I run out of things to write about? What if....?

Well, you know where those doubts were coming from.

I woke early, really early, the next morning with a start. (Usually I'm swimming up out of unconsciousness.) What had I done? I forgot to pray before I clicked those final OKs! I forgot to ask the Lord to bless it!

Now came the justification. *My* justification. I thought back to praying weeks ago... before starting this whole thing. I remembered praying before writing my first blog. I always pray before writing anything... or at least remember part way through when nothing seems to be working right.

There was a picture in my parents' living room when I was growing up. It was Jesus knocking at the door. That was always a puzzlement to me. Why would He need permission to go through a door? Who was on the other side?

That picture came to mind again that morning. I know it's not about faith. Who would open the door to a complete stranger, someone whose voice is unrecognizable? If He is to be believed when He says, "Lo, I am with you always!" (Matt. 28:20 KJV), why did He even need to come in? Does He need me to open that door for Him? Really?

No, it's about me. I need to open that door and acknowledge His presence in whatever I am doing. Whether it's in a song, a shout, a cry for help, a quietly breathed "Thank You"... I'm the one who benefits from this, not Him. That face in the picture of Jesus at the door is full of patience and forgiveness... for me. I'm not always patient and forgiving... especially with myself.

I had my moments with the Lord that morning, finally. I hadn't intended to blog again so soon, but this couldn't wait. I sat down... and the words began to flow.

Will the music of my life try again to drown out His knocking? Most assuredly. Will I hear His voice again and acknowledge His presence? That's a promise. Not mine, but His.

I'm Losing It!

Beep... Beep... (silence).

Try as hard as I could, I heard nothing. As my mind raced to catch up with my heart, I wondered if I should just lie. Stupid idea.

"Let's try that again."

Beep... Beep... (silence).

A few minutes later my doctor looked at the results and calmly said, "Nothing to be alarmed about. These things happen."

Are you kidding me? My hearing? I hear fine. I hear birds, the traffic outside my window, conversations, music... Music! What if I never hear music again? What if...? Stop it! This is now, today. I have arthritis beginning in the bones of my middle ear. They aren't picking up certain high frequencies. That's all.

From all of the physiology and audiology classes associated with my minor in speech pathology, I knew how this could affect me in the future. But this was now. Was it affecting my life?

Certainly my husband had noticed. We were checking our calendar and I commented that we couldn't accept an invitation for the third of February because we already had a commitment. He assured me that he had said the *first*, not the *third*. I realized that the two words contained any number of confusing sounds.

It happened again later that week. This time it was at choir practice, a public forum, not a private conversation. I thought I heard someone ask to go over one place in the music again, but I heard wrong. It wasn't because I wasn't paying attention. I heard one sound for another, or maybe I didn't hear a sound at all. (I told my choir I could *still* hear wrong notes and off-pitch blending, so they were *not* off the hook!)

Certain sounds are difficult to distinguish, even for people with normal hearing. That's why we have to spell VOGELSANG "V" as in Victor, "O", "G" as in girl, "E", "L", "S" as in Sam, "A", "N" as in Nancy, "G" as in girl when we talk with someone on the phone. Otherwise we get mail addressed to the BODELFAMD family. It's the high frequency sounds that make all the difference. For someone like me, this is going to be a problem.

Now I'm not looking for pity. We're not there yet. But I am now walking in shoes I never realized I would own so soon... shoes others have been wearing for years. I realize now how important it is for *me* to face someone I'm talking to so they can watch *my* lips and better "hear" the delicate difference between *my* "t" and "d". We're in this together now.

Another gentle reminder from God... I should never be too tired or busy to be patient with someone who has difficulty with anything I take for granted. I know my Lord never is with me. Patiently and lovingly my Shepherd guides me as I struggle to follow the "paths of righteousness" (Ps. 23:3 KJV), forgiving me when I stumble and then gently lifting me up.

The day may come when I need to get some help, and I hope I can gracefully turn that corner. If not, I trust someone will be kind enough to say to me, "Sweetie, it's time. You're losing it."

Lessons from Maude

"Can I braid your hair?"

What a strange request to get at church! For some time now I'd been watching this woman with the penetrating... no, *piercing* eyes... whose smile seemed forced and out of place on her stern face. What did she REALLY want to do to me?

Tentatively I agreed to drive to her place the following Saturday. That's when things weren't quite so busy on the farm, she told me.

Winding down an east Tennessee country road a week later, I was still pondering this strange invitation. But then Maude warmly greeted me in her shirtwaist dress and eagerly welcomed me into her home. A short time later her gentle hands weaved through my hair, thick and halfway down my back.

"I used to do this for my daughter. I love French braids."

No longer did the situation seem strange. She wanted to do something special for her pastor's wife. Something she enjoyed doing. We were bonded in a wonderful way from that day on.

My husband and I had been in our first parish only a month, and I was now learning the ways of being a pastor's wife, things they hadn't mentioned at the seminary. I took to heart the phrase, "We are here to serve, not be served." I was raised with that mantra, my parents expecting everyone to pitch in to do his or her part. Slackers were frowned on and rightfully so. I kept my eyes open for ways to serve in this new congregation and eagerly jumped in with willing hands.

And then there was Maude...

First it was helping me make curtains for the parsonage. Then after Carrie Anne was born, bringing little dresses made from her leftover material and lovingly tatted around the collar. If you don't know about tatting, it is a delicate, handmade lacing that is usually reserved for only the best. Her gift was always the best.

I learned about the ways of a Southern farm wife. Maude invited Carrie Anne and her friend Jill to toddle around the farm checking out the chickens and cows and laughing through wheelbarrow rides, courtesy of her husband Mac. When Mac was too sick to work, Maude took on his heavy chores but never missed a Sunday service. She nodded off, too exhausted to think, but spending time with her Lord and soaking in the love of her church family.

One obvious lesson I learned from Maude was not to allow my first impressions to determine someone's heart. But more importantly I learned the value of being a gracious receiver of gifts. I now understood why Jesus allowed those around Him to serve Him. It was because He understood their joy in giving. I needed this new insight.

There are times when we are hungry to be served. Times when we are sick... grieving... lonely. But then there are times when people just want to give to us.

I learned to give back the joy of receiving, even when the gift wasn't exactly what I needed or wanted. The school child's wilted rose bud I proudly wore all day pinned to my shirt. The second helping of homemade fruitcake I choked down as I smiled at the ninety-year-old grandmother. The candy dish I knew I would never use, already in my mind choosing a friend who would love it. Yet my thank you was still enthusiastic. Sometimes it's important to just not suck the joy out of someone else's giving... serving *them* by being graciously grateful.

The Sunday following that first visit with Maude, I carefully tidied up my beautiful French braids and wore my new style to church. I could see her joy and pride at the compliments on her gift to me.

Years later when I looked into her searching eyes, clouded with dementia, I knew the gift *she* would soon joyfully receive... the loving gentleness of her Savior's pierced hands stroking her hair, wiping away the clouds, and welcoming His servant home.

I Can Do This!

"What do you mean I'm not qualified to teach? I am credentialed in three states, and I'm already an experienced teacher. I have degrees in English and education from a highly recognized university."

"I'm sorry but California doesn't acknowledge any of those as qualifications to teach in this state."

Having a job was not an option for me. Soon after our move to California it became clear that we needed two incomes to sustain our family and to plan for our children's future education. Teaching was the obvious choice because it would allow me to have work hours similar to our children's school days. Besides, I was already a trained teacher... or so I thought.

The woman from the school district wasn't being unkind. In fact she was more than sympathetic. However, by the time I left her office I had a load of instructions and a list of tasks to accomplish that were overwhelming. Transcripts to submit for scrutiny. Tests to take. Classes to pass. An entire year of school called "The Fifth Year." I looked down the path stretching before me and could barely make out the distant finish line. Meanwhile I consoled myself that at least they would let me substitute... *after* I passed the state competency test of course.

Now was the time to bring out that favorite Scripture of mine: "I can do all things through Him who strengthens me." (Phil. 4:13 NAS) I sat down with my husband and made out my plan on his ever-trusty yellow legal pad. This was going to take awhile, but together we... my husband, my children, my Lord, and I... could do it.

You know, that verse is a great comfort when working towards a goal. The problem comes when the rules keep changing. Every time I thought I was "qualified" to get a real job, there was another certification needed to make me even *more* qualified. More classes, more tests. I became convinced that the State of California was just dreaming up requirements to frustrate me. Part time jobs weren't going to cut it. I needed a long-term position I could count on for a steady paycheck.

When "they" keep moving the finish line farther down the road, it's tough not to lose hope. I was starting to lose my confidence, my sense of *me*.

Quietly the Lord lifted my downcast spirit by showing me another verse, one I had read before but really needed at this particular moment: "[We are] strengthened with all power, according to His glorious might, for the attaining of all steadfastness and patience, joyously giving thanks to the Father, who has qualified us to share in the inheritance of the saints in light" (Col. 1:11-12 NAS). Okay, there was the word "strength" again. But now it was coupled with "steadfastness" and "patience." Oh, the "P" word. He was encouraging me to keep going.

The word that leaped out at me, however, was "qualified." My Lord had *already* qualified me... declared me "fit for a special purpose." My self worth did not depend on the world's standards. I didn't need the State of California to certify me as a valued person. It didn't matter what *they* thought I was qualified to do. What mattered was what He knew I was qualified for... His special purpose! I thanked him for His validation.

In the end I did get a teaching position that lasted fifteen years. Ironically it was at a school that didn't require ANY of the classes, tests, or credentials I now had in my job-searching arsenal. That's okay. All of those years of extra study benefitted me, and those whom I've taught, in countless ways.

And the best thing I learned? The certification that I really needed, I had all along. I was already a certified child of the Living God!

I didn't have to take any classes or tests. My Savior passed all of those requirements for me and nailed the final exam.

And when I tried to tell Him "I can do this!" He firmly but gently said "No you can't."

Whose Idea Was This Anyway?

"Help! I've been hijacked! At least my idea has been."
I looked squarely into my friend Jackie's eyes and told her I needed her help to derail the plans of a woman at my church.

Her face barely masked the horror she was feeling as she calmly said, "You need to pray about this... and for her. I'll be praying for you... and your attitude."

Pray? My attitude? I'm right! I don't need to pray!

It had been just a few months since I had attended Jackie's weekend conference on women's ministry. Our brand new congregation had almost no established ministries. This was a perfect time to implement the plan laid out by Jackie and the other speakers to bring new life and meaning to this important area of the church. She had encouraged me to go for it. And now she was putting up her hand to stop me?

An older woman at our mission church had just announced *her* plan to start up a women's group that would oversee all of the activities associated with the ladies of the congregation. It was the same framework used by countless churches over the years. To me it was just the same old, same old. This couldn't be happening! Not with all of the new possibilities for ministry *I* had been hoping to try out. She and I were on a collision course.

Don't you hate it when someone... a boss, a coworker, a group project member... "steals" your idea, either knowingly or unknowingly? As they claim it for their own, no one even notices you anymore. I'm not talking about patents and intellectual property. No. These are the everyday ideas that just emerge from a discussion or planning session. And it becomes unbearable when they change your idea to something no longer resembling the original and then criticize you when it doesn't work! Well, I wasn't going to take the blame for this failure that was bound to happen!

I grudgingly began my prayer. It wasn't the I'm-sorry-for-my-behavior one. It was the foot stomping, I-want-my-way one. The Lord wasn't surprised. He never is. He just started working on my attitude... and my heart... in His ever-patient way.

Many years after this tirade, I sat next to a teacher friend who was retiring. We were listening to accolades for a ministry she had organized and promoted at the school. She whispered to me that she was so embarrassed because it actually had been my idea. I assured her that without her tireless efforts to implement it, the idea would never have reached so many students' hearts. It was okay.

How important is recognition anyway? What do we want? A sash of badges to wear so we can point to each one? "And this one I got when I came up with that wonderful idea for..." Is it important that our ideas are noticed? When people know we've been passed over for recognition and they now are watching for our reaction, do we mirror that verse, "Love does not insist on its own way"? (1 Cor. 13:5 RSV) Then again, do we recognize that it never was *our* idea in the first place?

My mother used to remind me that what's most important is that something gets done, not who gets the credit for it. Oh, but Mom, it *is* important to give the credit where it's due. "We are His workmanship, created in Christ Jesus for good works (good ideas), *which God prepared beforehand...*" (Eph. 2:10 NAS). Oh... so that women's ministry thing was His idea all along.

Over the years, men and women in our congregation have had ministry ideas they were excited about... prayer quilts, encouragement to mothers of preschoolers, flowers to shut ins, support to those who have lost jobs, and many other wonderful ways to serve. The ideas have been endless and no one is worried about taking credit. That "same old, same old" I thought was never going to work? It turned out to be someone's comfort zone, someone's joy. It has flourished.

She never knew we were on a collision course. Thankfully I never confronted her. I had good counsel and guidance from my Lord and from those He sent to me.

Each Christmas when I sat at the piano in church, I was the closest person to one of her best ideas... one that continues to live on even now that she's gone. The Chrismons that decorate the tree talked to me... reminding me of how close I came to missing out on a wonderful friend and teammate in one of God's best ideas... preparing the two of us for good works to glorify Him.

I Can... But Should I?

"Down it firefighter!"

My husband urged me to finish the last few swallows of my root beer float. I knew if I did, there was a danger it wouldn't stay down. My goodness! I've eaten myself sick!

A new Souplantation had recently opened closer to us in Escondido. These restaurants are one of our favorite places to spend a twosome dinner out. Each time we go, my husband, who has no sense of culinary adventure, begins with a healthy serving of salads and then scoops up his usual three or four bowls of clam chowder and a plate of blueberry muffins. I enjoy sampling all of the soups and relishing the foods my family refuses to eat at home... beets and tapioca pudding, for example. I must admit that when we eat out I actually enjoy ordering certain items from the menu just to watch them gag.

But here we were in the all-you-can-stuff-in-your-mouth arena. I wasn't really that hungry since I had enjoyed lunch a few hours earlier. However, the soup varieties enticed me to sample four different bowls. And they were all delicious. There was even a new whipped maple butter to slather on my cornbread and muffins. The tapioca pudding called to me, and I gladly answered.

Now I was feeling a little uncomfortable to say the least, but my empty soda glass stared at me. After all, we had already paid for that glass. My mother's voice reached out to me from my childhood.

"You took it. Now eat it!"

I waddled over to the soft serve ice cream, filled my glass half full, and topped it off with root beer.

Just because you can do it doesn't mean it's a good thing. Those words paraphrased from First Corinthians 10:23 came to me as I nursed a very bad stomachache at home that evening. My husband kept reminding me of all I had eaten, totally amazed at my ability to gorge myself.

"And then I couldn't believe it when you..."

The food commercials on TV made it even worse. I hadn't listened to my common sense, and now I was paying for it dearly. Sometimes I really do let myself get out of control.

There are times when we don't listen to our Lord... or people He sends to us... as we forge ahead into reckless behavior. Sometimes the result is pain to ourselves, physical pain. But even worse is the pain we cause from not what goes into our mouths but what comes out.

Jesus warned of this danger in Matthew 15:18 when He spoke of the heartache our words can cause. This is not a passing hurt but often one that has trouble healing with time... or never does. Just because I can say it... and it may even be true... doesn't mean I should.

I've had more than my share of those mistakes. Usually it's when I feel *so* right and *so* justified in my behavior. Later the battle rages in my mind and soul. My virtuous attitude fights for victory even as I am trying to suppress my desire to be vindicated.

That's when I need to remember to seek my Lord's firm limits on my behavior as I go to Him in prayer... asking Him for strength to not repeat my careless words and begging for healing for whatever damage I have caused.

Fortunately I didn't finish off that float, and I made it home to the couch, moaning all the way. I'm not sure what will happen on future visits to this wonderful restaurant.

However, if you should find me standing in front of the tapioca pudding with my head bowed and eyes closed, feel free to whisper in my ear, "You really shouldn't."

But You're So Good At It!

"So... when is the first choir practice?"

I blankly looked into her face and said I didn't know.

"Well, *you're* the choir director!" she continued.

"Really? Who told you that?"

"Pastor K."

"He did? Oh...."

Me? Choir director? I didn't know this was part of the deal. I've only directed children's choirs. This means I REALLY need to know what I'm doing.

It was our first Sunday at our new mission church in California and already I was realizing that this would be a totally new experience from our first two congregations. Before, when we had arrived on the scene, I just had to discover how I would fit into the ministries already established, helping out usually in music and education. However, the founding pastor of this mission had found out I was a musician and decided I would be the music director. Now I would be part of the ground floor, developing and growing all kinds of opportunities for people to serve, especially in music.

I had spent years taking music lessons, music classes, singing in choirs. I knew a lot about music... but this was a different angle. I had never really been in charge. And now I had to face that first choir. All those adults looking to me... at me... expecting great things.

There was no music. I had to choose it, order it, figure out how to teach it. What do I do with my arms when I actually have to lead them?

Actually that wasn't an issue to begin with since I had to play the piano and direct at the same time. I could hide behind my dear old friend and peer over the top from my bench.

Then came bells... and children's choir... and a praise team.

My husband kept saying, "But you're so good at it!"

And besides, there really wasn't anyone at the church who knew more about music than I did. Or at least anyone who would admit it and be willing to lead.

I learned to fake my confidence. It was scary at first, but the Lord kept leading me to resources and showing me the path to building our music program. Pretty soon I started believing I could do it, and the Lord and I were off and running.

Sometimes we are reluctant to answer God's call. Like Moses we have all sorts of excuses... I'm not good enough... I've got this terrible handicap... What if I fail?... Can't you get someone else to do it?

Other times we become the leader in different ways... the one who becomes an example for others: "You're always there for me." "I know I can always count on you." "You have such faith!" "You're so strong!"

People look to us... our children, our coworkers, our friends, our students, our family... the list grows longer. The pressure is on to be "the one" everyone looks to, depends on. At first our egos say they are right. But our honest self-reflection mirrors the truth.

And then come the personal tsunamis that roll over us. We try to prop ourselves up with a confidence that is shaky and often hollow. It's bad enough when we lean on flawed external props, but when we use ourselves... when we dig down for that power within us, the strength that everyone tells us we have... we come up empty handed.

These are the times when no matter what people say or think, we aren't going to be able to pull it off. Times when our faith feels so inadequate or doesn't even seem to be there. Times when we feel we will collapse.

And we should... into our Savior's arms.

"When every earthly prop gives way, He then is all my hope and stay" (from "My Hope Is Built on Nothing Less").

That's the part God enjoys the most... when we desperately cry out for help with the Psalmist... when we finally admit we aren't so strong after all... we aren't "the one."

The Scriptures are full of flawed people that the Lord took just as they were and made into His leaders, His faith heroes... some important... and some just ordinary... like us.

He has this wonderful way of turning our lives around and heading us in the right direction, strengthening us with His power, encouraging and forgiving us along the way.

And really... He's so good at it!

You Know How I Feel

I inched closer to the edge of the Grand Canyon... fifty feet away... summoning my courage to peer over. Glancing to my left I locked eyes with another terrified woman who was mirroring my every move.

She called out, "You too? Thank goodness! I thought I was losing my mind!"

It didn't lessen our fear, but there was a certain comfort knowing we weren't alone.

My high school English teacher always stressed the difference between sympathy and empathy. She talked about sympathy as being something "next to" and empathy being "within." It's the difference between feeling sorry something has happened to someone and actually internalizing the sorrow.

Sometimes we can only hold people close because we feel for them. At other times our experiences allow us to "walk in someone else's shoes" when they are hurting.

Years ago I realized how closely I could walk in those "shoes" as a dear friend clutched my hand and searched my eyes. Surrounded by a group of women gathered for a Bible study in a friend's home, she was having a full-blown panic attack. As I described what she must be feeling... the out-of-control... the pounding heart... the urge to flee... I could feel a slight give, a moment of recognition, a welcome relief.

"You know how I feel," she whispered.

I did know *what* she was feeling because of my unreasonable fear of heights. I have experienced panic attacks in various lofty locations.

I could relive with her all of those unexplainable, uncontrollable emotions and physical impulses. But did I really know *how* she felt?

How much can we really be empathetic? When someone loses a spouse or a child or a parent or a friend, we can say it has happened to us too. But can we truly feel what they are feeling? I don't think so.

We can't relive those special memories they shared with their loved one. We can't feel the same regret for their lost opportunities. We don't have the same mental and emotional strengths or weaknesses they have... those things that help them cope or leave them floundering. As much compassion as we are feeling for them, we can't really walk in their shoes. And they can't walk in ours.

I think about how we are assured that Jesus understands us completely. He was tempted as we are. He felt the same human pains, pleasures, and needs we do.

But then I sometimes wonder if He really *does* understand. He didn't go through childbirth. He didn't watch a loved one die because of a reckless driver. He didn't experience the horror of war or a natural disaster. Those things weren't part of His earthly experience. How can He really be empathetic? How can He really walk in my shoes? They are mine, not His.

And then I remember Psalm 139. He knows everything about me... what I'm thinking even before I think it... what I will do before I do it. He is everywhere I go and in every emotion I feel. When I am in the darkness of depression, it is His daylight that is there... even when I don't always recognize it. When I can't sleep at night or when I am ecstatic with joy over one of my children's accomplishments, He feels it with me. He is "intimately acquainted with all my ways" (v. 3 NAS). He didn't have to experience it first hand when He was on earth because He experiences all things... in us... with us. He's in my shoes at the same time I am.

That's the real joy in His assurance,

The fear may still be there, but there is great comfort knowing I am never alone... and knowing He really does know how I feel.

No, But I Could Have

I opened the parsonage door to the beaming, eager face of one of my friends from church.

"I have a big bushel of peaches in the car for you!"

"Oh... I really don't think I'll need a whole bushel," I replied.

"You don't have to eat them all right now. You should can them," she suggested.

"I don't know how."

"I'll show you how," she offered.

Suddenly I had visions of my mother standing over a steaming pot of sterilizing Mason jars.

"No thank you."

Her smile vanished. "Why not?"

Calmly I told her I didn't want one more thing to feel guilty about not doing. Her face relaxed into a grin as she knowingly nodded.

—⚜—

Early in my life I started to realize that there were just too many choices for how I could spend my hours. I learned how to read, play the piano, ski, sew, knit, sing, paint, study, talk on the phone, go to church... the list was always there, each activity vying for my time. Sometimes one thing claimed a higher place over the others depending on my interests or responsibilities. But there was no way possible to fit everything into my life. When I kept adding things, the guilt over neglecting certain skills and tasks would become overwhelming.

Sometimes our choices seem set in stone. Certainly there are days and seasons of our lives when our choices are really obligations, especially if we want to be responsible people. We need an income to provide for our needs. We can't abandon our children, parents or friends who truly depend on us. These are tough times, when we seem to be on overload. That's when prayers for wisdom and strength become vital.

Other times we run the risk of becoming a prisoner to our choices. When we moved to southern California the range of options for our family's time seemed limitless. The weather was almost always cooperative. There was very little "down time." Sports didn't have seasons. They were year round. And overlapping! Other choices competed for our attention and our children's time. Scouting, dance, music, theme parks, cultural celebrations, church. Again, the endless list. All of them were great choices, but we knew we couldn't do them all… and stay focused on what was important. Before this lifestyle got too out of control with commitments, we knew we had to rescue some time for just the five of us… alone together. And we did.

A few years ago a wonderful school principal told my graduate class that there are only so many hours in each teaching day and we all had the same restrictions on our time. Well that wasn't news, but her advice was a new twist for me. She said that we will always come across some good idea or creative lesson that we really want to do but don't think we have the time for. It is impossible to squeeze any more into the day or add any more time. It was up to us, if we really felt this new idea was important, to evaluate what we were already doing and get rid of something that wasn't as valuable to our day. And let it go! No guilt about not doing it all. Do what is most important and revisit our priorities on a regular basis.

Actually this wasn't her idea, but she didn't know it. Psalm 90:12 asks the Lord to "teach us to number our days, that we may gain a heart of wisdom." Now in this hurried-up world it's more like teach us to number our *hours*. But the idea is still the same. Help me to be wise in the way I use my time, my hours, my days. And keep me from feeling guilty about not doing it all! Help me to filter out the things that aren't so important to leave those that make my life most meaningful.

—⚜—

In the days before homogenized milk, we had to shake the bottle to mix in the cream. When everything was once again calm, we watched the richness rise to the top.

When I take the time to reflect on my "shaken-up life"... asking for the Lord's wisdom... He calms my spirit and I can watch the rich choices rise above all the others.

In the past, when someone asked me if I had knitted a sweater or made a creative dessert, I used to flounder in my guilt about not measuring up to their expectations. But now the Lord has taught me to say with a smile, "No, but I could have."

Our Lord Jesus had many, many people and choices vying for His time in His three short years of ministry. He knew His days on this earth were limited, and He had many options open to Him as to how He would spend them. Thankfully He wasn't like me... easily distracted by the world and all it has to offer.

On His way to the cross He could have turned His back on me and walked away. He had that choice.

But then His voice whispers to me... assuring me of how important I am... "I could have, but I didn't."

Lessons from Jim

"Are you ever going to eat that?" I wondered as I watched my friend's fork hover between his mouth and the plate.

He was so engrossed in conversations around the table, focusing on each person's comments, that we were finished eating long before his plate of food had grown cold. No wonder He didn't have trouble with weight gain!

Jim was my husband's boyhood friend, the one who was the wise, cautious counterpoint to Bill's impulsive exuberance in those years when the Lord was fashioning their personalities.

Jim could make anyone feel special. He had this incredible ability to make you feel you were the most important person in the room. When he talked with you it was as if he had all the time in the world. He would have been a wonderful priest, but instead God decided that he would make the best husband for Bunnie.

However, the Lord still had great plans to use Jim in His kingdom. It didn't take long for Jim to see the path to service that opened to him. He would still be ministering, but in a different way.

For twenty-eight years Jim was the first to greet grieving families at the cemetery, helping them through those difficult but necessary decisions. And he was the last to say goodbye after their loved one had been lowered into the grave and they needed to move on in their lives. He reached countless people with our Lord's love and grace.

When we last visited Jim and Bunnie in their home it had been many, long, busy years since we had seen them... years devoted to our children's lives and our own careers. Nothing had changed between us... yet everything had changed.

Jim's body was abandoning his mind through ALS, better known as Lou Gehrig's disease. As we chatted with him it was obvious he was walking the tightrope between life and death... struggling with each breath... agonizing over the loss of control of his once fine-tuned body.

There was another struggle going on, however. Trying to make sense out of what was happening. Finding purpose in the midst of anger, sorrow, frustration, sadness. As days and nights melted together, Jim had a lot of time to think... and pray.

"To live is Christ and to die is gain!" (Phil. 1:21) played itself out before our eyes. Wanting to leave his suffering behind him, Jim still allowed himself to be used by God in unexpected ways. Still amazed by God. This is what we saw and heard.

We were still the most important people in the room, but this time Jim was doing all the talking. Reminding us of his blessings. Telling about how many people he had been able to share God's love with... in the past and even now at the end of his life. Assuring us of his confidence in the Lord's promise of salvation. Thanking us for our friendship and love.

Many people expressed their concern for Jim in those last months. He said he was surprised by how many told him how kind he had been to them. He didn't understand what they meant. But I did. It was his ability to focus on who I was and what I needed. He was a master at it.

We prayed for a miracle that would reverse the course of Jim's life. However, the alternative, when it came, was truly gain.

As the tightrope dissolved and Jim walked into his Savior's arms, what could compare to hearing our Lord's voice say... "Relax. We have all the time in the world... and you, Jim, are the most important person in the room."

Listening to Voices

I stared down at the knife in my right hand and the slimy bird in the other. From the corner of my eye I could see my three preschoolers quietly sitting around the kitchen table keeping themselves busy with play dough and crayons. Sigh. Another chicken to cut up to save money. Another dinner to fix. Another day of routine. Another…

A voice interrupted my thought trail.

"Since when did *you* become so everyday?" it challenged. "What has happened to you?"

Resolutely I dropped the knife, stuck my hand up that chicken, and began to dance and sing it around the edge of the sink. My children dissolved into hysterical giggles as they joined me in my silliness.

―――

There are times in our lives when we lose our voice. Now this isn't because of laryngitis, which I have suffered from periodically. No, this is the voice that is the essence of who we are. Ruth Culham in her book *6+1 Traits of Writing* speaks so eloquently about voice. I could actually hear her voice in my ear as I taught my students that it was the most important aspect of their writing.

But it is also the imprint of ourselves on whatever we do. The music in our lives that holds everything together. It isn't emotion; however, it's found in how we express every one of our emotions.

If people don't hear our voice, then something is definitely missing. Perhaps we are tired, bored, stretched to the max, or feeling trapped. Those are the enemies of the voice each of us has within us.

As a young teen I remember trying out different "voices" to see who I really was. Serious? Silly? Carefree? Focused? But each time they had a hollow ring. They weren't really voices. Only moods. Fortunately the Lord blessed me with a mother whose voice encouraged me to embrace opportunities and take risks. She and I struggled... sometimes together and sometimes at odds with one another... as I discovered my voice and practiced using it.

Later in college I found that my voice wasn't always appreciated. As an English major I had countless writing assignments that I tried to put my own imprint on... connecting with my own experiences and with what I was learning in other classes. My classic attempt was "Gestalt as Applied to *A Tale of a Tub*." It combined my newfound psychology knowledge with Jonathan Swift. As I leafed through the graded paper I saw there were very few red marks. Ah... a possible A? However, my professor was not amused. She said my line of argument was "not characteristic of 18th century thought" and gave me a B. She did say that even though the approach was "less than convincing," it *was* ingenious. Oh, she liked my voice! I'll take an A for that!

A few years ago I had the good fortune to, literally, sit at the feet of Ray Bradbury, that wonderful American author. Since I was a late arrival to the session, I lost out on a chair but gained a seat on the floor... right in front!

Among the many bits of wisdom for writers, he interjected his thoughts about the appreciation for life he had gained in his almost 90 years. He repeated more than once his insistence to "Do what you love, and love what you do!"

Now it is certainly true that we can't always do what we love. That sounds like an endless vacation with endless possibilities. There are limits to our resources, time, and abilities. Even so, one of the true joys in life is when we are able to connect what we love with what we do.

It is, however, possible to love what we are doing. Or at least find *something* to love about it, even if it's that accomplishment at the end of a particularly unpleasant task. (Cleaning the toilet or the grill comes to mind.)

In our daily routine of life... the attention to our jobs and families... the responsibilities that come with each hour... even cutting up chicken... those are the times to infuse our voice into whatever we are doing. Bring the ordinary to life!

At the same time I need to be mindful of how I interject my voice into the lives of others. It is my connection with them, so I need to be sensitive to how I am sharing and making sense out of our experience together. That's the writer being aware of her audience. That's a Christian being aware of her witness.

As great as Bradbury's presentation was, he still had some quirky ideas. His voice wasn't always connecting with me because I could hear Another's voice reminding me to be discerning.

It's my Savior's voice that assures me each day that I can trust Him. For He promises, "My sheep hear My voice, and I know them, and they follow Me... and no one shall snatch them out of My hand" (John 10:27-28 NAS).

This is the Voice I pray I am internalizing. The Voice that I am confident can make everything I do and say hold together... so that each day is fresh... and also joyful!

Don't Waste My Time!

My eyes widened and the blush crept up my face as I stared at the steamy passage I was reading. Quickly I looked around to see if anyone was peeking over my shoulder. My goodness!

Across the wide-bodied jet my newest friend Amy calmly sat next to the far window. She barely knew me... and on top of that... I was her Pastor's wife! She picked this book out for *me?*

By the time we reached Munich on our way to Israel, I had finished *The Notebook* by Nicholas Sparks. It was the beginning of many more wonderful reads Amy would share with me.

―⚊―

When I was a young child our home was a library. In the living room my mom had shelves of books from her book club. We had shelves of books in our bedrooms. The one purchase my mother never refused me was another treasured Golden Book. I read them over and over, growing in confidence in my new ability to escape into a different world. As I gained in my reading skill, my older sisters' collections of *The Bobbsey Twins, Nancy Drew,* and *Cherry Ames,* along with classics like *Tom Sawyer, The Secret Garden,* and *Heidi,* enchanted me for hours.

And then book reports came along and spoiled it all. The light turned off in my head. I was now into "school" reading. Usually we read what we were told. When I went to the library no one helped find a book just for me or told me about authors who were great writers. I just picked the shortest book with the biggest print... one that I could finish quickly and get the report over with. No one chatted with me about the book or shared insights about how wonderfully it was written.

Not much changed over the years as I continued to read whatever were considered "classics" by my various teachers and English professors. There were the never-ending quizzes... and tests... and writing responses... and papers. This was analyzing, not chatting. At times it was pure drudgery. It's amazing I stayed with it! But I felt I was absorbing something... and I kept hearing a whisper that there was more behind this veil.

One year during my husband's seminary studies, I worked as a secretary not far from the public library. Since I wasn't teaching and had no papers to grade in the evenings, I had lots of free time. I hurried over to the library on my lunch break to choose books by what I considered "contemporary" authors... Hemingway, Steinbeck... the old familiars from school. What refreshment not to have to write a report! Now this was fun again! There was still no one to chat and share with, but at least I wasn't wasting my time reading an author I wasn't sure of.

Years later my children reintroduced me to the world of children's books. My, how well written some of the new ones were! And the old classics from my childhood had stood the test of time... even after the 100th reading. Well, maybe not *The Bobbsey Twins*. I must have lived a pretty dull life to have once found their adventures fascinating.

When I returned to teaching, I realized that I had few answers when my middle school students asked me for book suggestions. However, I soon became fast friends with the school librarian, who was eager to share her abundant knowledge of adolescent literature and great authors for kids. Her recommendations were never a waste of my time. We chatted away and shared our appreciation for these wonderful writers. The books on the shelves of that library turned into a familiar field of joyful hours of reading... reading I could then pass on to my students. Over the years I became the go-to teacher for reading ideas in the schools where I taught. (And, by the way, I never assigned a book report.)

Leaving My Guilt at the Cross

But I was an adult... and my daughter told me that it was time I read some age appropriate literature. Time to grow up! Oh no... back to those shelves in the library with the dusty classics... or the bookstores where names and titles swam before my eyes. I didn't want to waste my time or money on a book that wasn't any good!

Enter Amy. Thank you, my dear! She was the friend who knew which books to load me down with at the bookstore, and who now gives me a list to put on my e-reader... the friend who loves to listen to me gushing over a particularly well-written section. She would *never* waste my time.

When I was a young child I loved stories from the Bible. My public school first grade teacher actually read to our class from my own favorite treasury of Bible stories. Imagine that!

But years later I would stare at the Bible the way I used to hesitate in front of those library shelves. Where to begin? I didn't want to waste my time. So I opened up to the familiar stories in Genesis and The Gospels and started there. Wondering what else happened to those people led me into other books... Acts, the Samuels. Wondering who these writers were and what else they wrote led me to Exodus and The Letters of the New Testament. And the journey continues...

Along the way I have had the joy of chatting with others about these wonderful writings in Bible classes and encounters. How wonderful to appreciate the great poetry of Isaiah and the Psalms... the rich words of John's gospel!

The best part, though, comes when I get to sit down alone with the Author by my side... in my mind... speaking to my heart. He points out passages that give me the words I need for that exact moment.

And spending time with Him in His Word... in His Books... in His Writing... is never a waste of my time. I always find something new... even after the 100th reading.

And I never have to write a report!

No, I Really Can't

"What is the next number in the series?"

I confidently filled in the circle with the correct answer and moved on to question two. Same question, different numbers. What? I have no clue.

As a good test taker I didn't dwell on my lack of knowledge but moved on to the next question... and the next... and the next. The numbers made no sense to me. I quickly scanned the test and realized I had no idea what I was doing. I quietly put down my pencil, closed my eyes, and waited for the time to expire. Obviously I wasn't going to be a computer programmer for the State of Illinois.

―∞―

My fourth grade teacher told my mother at the end-of-the-year conference, "Christine can be anything she wants to be."

Well, that's a pretty heady comment for a ten-year-old to hear. Wow! Anything? My mind began to dream as my mom gave her usual "You'll never know what you can do unless you try" encouragement.

Of course it didn't take long for reality to set in. My pigeon toes and flat feet were not suited for ballet. I wasn't "fast" at much of anything... running, swimming, skiing. My poor eyesight would keep me from becoming an aviatrix. Physically I just couldn't cut it for many options my teacher had assured me I could do.

As freshmen entering high school, my friend Diane and I sat next to each other taking various aptitude tests that would help guide us toward success. I relished the puzzles and gears. She flew through the "clerical speed and accuracy" sections. She would make a great secretary. I was supposed to become an engineer, architect, or dentist. However, trigonometry and chemistry would later discourage me from pursuing those careers. Even though I did well in those subjects, I just couldn't get excited about them. By the way, Diane *did* become a fantastic executive secretary.

I learned to refocus my efforts during those years. Instead of speed, I aimed at accuracy. Instead of sprinting, I concentrated on endurance... sticking with something until it was finished, and encouraging others to keep at it too. Doing my best at what I *could* do.

This attitude helped me make some wise choices. I played the Chopin waltzes that were more my speed, literally! I dropped a water ski instead of continuing to strain my left leg in vain attempts to get up on one. I could enjoy the recreation of sports instead of the competition, the pleasure of doing something well even if it didn't earn me a prize.

I now had a better approach to appreciating God's blessings. He does promise to give each of us gifts, according to His purpose, His love, and His grace. He chooses them especially for each one of us. And gives us the opportunity to use them and improve on them.

Wishing and hoping got me nowhere. Wistfully envying others' gifts and accomplishments only bred resentment. I needed eyes that focused on how differently gifted people worked together, complemented one another. That gave me a better understanding of how the world worked and more importantly how God's people lived abundantly. That's the best part of God's giving plan... that we concentrate on using our gifts to build up His church... His people.

As a teacher I made it my goal each year to find out what each student was good at. I knew there was a gift in there somewhere, even if they didn't think they had one. I needed to help them discover how they could channel those gifts and use them to succeed. My reward was watching a particularly discouraged child beam with pride at an answer no one else had thought of or a skill no one else knew she had.

My fourth grade teacher helped my confidence as a young child, but he didn't quite have it right. I can't be anything I want to be. I can't make decent scalloped potatoes. I can't be perfect.

Do you remember as a child trying for just one day, one hour, or one minute to do everything right to avoid getting "yelled at" by your parents? It was impossible. I had this mistaken idea that the day would come when I would have it all figured out and wouldn't make mistakes any more. Well, that day didn't come. I couldn't do it then, and I can't do it now... no matter how much time and effort I put into it.

Thank goodness God didn't "yell at" me for something I couldn't do. He knew I could never live up to His standard of perfection. Not that I don't give it my best effort! But I will always fall short... and He knows it.

That's why His Son gave me that perfect gift, His perfect Self on the cross dying for my sins.

And then he showed me the other side of the gift... the abundant life of abilities and blessings from Him... to use and enjoy to His glory... now and forever.

Now that's a prize to be proud of!

I Didn't Really Mean It!

It was my husband's birthday and I had prepared a special dinner with just him in mind. I told him to close his eyes as I set the lovingly prepared plate before him.

"Surprise!"

"What's this?"

"Carrots."

"You *know* I *hate* carrots."

"But these are Deena's glazed carrots. The ones you complimented her on... again and again... when we were at her house. I got the recipe just for you."

He groaned, "I was just being polite. I didn't really *mean* it!"

Years later my husband rushed home to tell me that he had found the perfect Christmas gift for his parents that year. He and his dad had been to a ballgame and had seen on the jumbo screen an ad for hot air balloon rides. Bill said that it looked like fun. And his dad agreed. A few weeks later his father called down to us that he really didn't mean it... as we waved goodbye to them... lifting into the air... their white-knuckled fingers gripping the side of the basket.

While we were visiting our daughter during her Peace Corps years in the Dominican Republic, she warned me to not compliment anyone on a picture in their home or they would take it right off the wall and give it to me. I found out later that this gifting phenomenon wasn't just a Latin cultural thing. When asked if I liked a particularly "colorful" Christmas decoration hanging in my neighbor's home, I politely said it was very pretty.

"Great! I was hoping you'd like it, because I made it just for you!"

That turned into one of those pass-me-on gifts, by the way.

Not meaning what you say can create some serious moments too. During my second year of teaching I had "called out" a junior high student for handing in a paper obviously copied from her friend. The next afternoon her mother accosted me for calling her daughter stupid. I didn't remember saying it and assured her I would never refer to a student as stupid.

"Oh *no*," she insisted. "You said, 'How could you be so stupid to think I would fall for something like that!'"

Oh, I guess I did say it. I told her that what I meant to say was, "How could you think *I* was so stupid that I would fall for something like that."

I apologized and said the words came out wrong. It didn't matter to her. Never mind her daughter was caught cheating. Never mind that we were in a school where Martin Luther's admonition to "put the best construction on everything" should have been heeded.

How many times have we said things we shouldn't have... left out the filter to thoughts that went directly from our minds to our tongues and bypassed our hearts? We say we didn't mean it... but sometimes we really did. What we are thinking slips out in anger and frustration. Sometimes we actually take the time to write it down and send it through the mail... or these days, through a text or an email. Later, instead of saying I didn't mean it, I have to lamely, but more honestly, admit that I shouldn't have said what I was thinking.

And then there is the receiving end of rude or hurtful comments. Some are justified in their content, but not in their delivery. Others are flaming arrows of unjust accusations. I have tried to put into practice the Lord's urging to turn the other cheek. It's so much more helpful in the long run. But sometimes it's really hard!

However, getting into a confrontation only fuels negative attitudes and thoughts on both sides. I find that when I give time for hearts to soften... time for reflection... time for retreat and even retraction and apology, I can often salvage a relationship... even a friendship that was put on hold for twenty-five years.

Leaving My Guilt at the Cross

And those that continue to carry the torch of animosity? The Lord gives me permission to wipe the dust off my feet and move on! He also encourages me to pray for them, but more importantly to ask for forgiveness for the thoughts I still have about them.

As children we were prone to strike out with words of "I hate you!" "I don't ever want to be your friend again!" Hopefully as adults we are learning to curb our emotions and keep our caustic comments in check.

Yet as grown-up children we are apt to strike out at our Heavenly Father with those same angry thoughts, especially when things aren't going "our way." Sometimes I can see myself pounding on His chest crying out, "It isn't fair!" And it doesn't matter if we shout out the actual words. He knows our thoughts. We can't hide our true feelings from Him. He knows we mean it.

Thankfully He gives us time to regret... retract... repent... and time for Him to renew us when we leave our hearts open to His touch. As far as the east is from the west we can watch our sinful words and thoughts fly from us. That's His promise.

I hear the words spoken from the cross... just for me... "Father forgive her."

And He really means it.

A Trio of Saints

"We'll miss you!" I assured the elderly woman at our church in Arkansas.

I had just met her that Sunday morning and was touched by her sadness at leaving. Against her wishes she was moving closer to her son so he could care for her.

What I meant as a passing kindness turned into a nightmare. No sooner had she settled into her new surroundings than she began to bombard me with requests for letters and phone calls. She even complained when the picture she demanded I send her wasn't recent enough.

"Why haven't you called me?" she would whine.

I had enough to keep my own relatives up to date on the latest family news. I finally resolved to simply ignore the neediness of this woman.

People with needs tug at my heart. People who are needy make me cringe.

—⚬—

"We'll miss you!"

Not too many years ago, all within the same month, three dear friends left this earth after long declines in their health. The hole in my heart will always be there.

All of them had needs. Candy lived with MS and then was hit by cancer. Jim had ALS. Ellen's ninety-year-old body gradually slowed down and finally said, "Enough!"

Yet none of them was needy... even as life's shade was being lowered. Candy had set aside her nursing career to raise her four boys and cheer on her husband. In the end she set aside her needs and pain and kept her focus on others, her smile lighting up the room as she chatted away, asking about others so she could pray for them.

Jim's urgent witnessing to those gathered around him consumed the last of his life ... a life that was numbered by days and then hours.

Right up to the end, Ellen continued her handwritten notes and brief-but-to-the-point phone calls of encouragement and concern.

Not one of them ever made me feel guilty for not *being* enough or *doing* enough for them. They allowed others to live their lives and cheered them on.

Cheering crowds are commonplace in our world... cheering the victories of teams and individuals... cheering newlyweds... cheering the end of wars... the end of evil.

A few weeks after my friends died I watched cheering crowds on my television screen. Many people expressed the mixed emotions I was feeling. It was the end of the mastermind of the 9-11 attack... a particularly odious man who was the antithesis of my three friends. Of course we were not sad at his passing. He will *not* be missed. And yet we are urged, no, commanded... to love our enemies. How difficult is that challenge!

I have mixed emotions when I read the passage from Psalm 116:15: "Precious in the sight of the Lord is the death of his faithful servants." I know the families of my friends felt relief that suffering had ended...

but they also experienced tremendous grief at their loss. Death is so very hard this side of heaven.

But as I read the entire psalm, the words clearly apply to my dear ones. All were ready to leave. All experienced a cheering throng of angels and sainted loved ones welcoming them home. There were no mixed emotions in that crowd. They were of one spirit.

I'll take the heavenly cheering section any day! The cheers for my Lord's victory over death and evil. The cheers that tell me I don't have to worry about being or doing enough. The cheers that remind me that His victory was just for my dear friends... and also for me.

If I Can, Why Can't You?

"Oh no! I'm out of milk and it's almost time for dinner!" I grabbed my three young children from their swings and sandbox, buckled them into the car, and headed for the grocery store.

"Hurry!"

Out of the car... into the store... up in the cart...

"Oh no! Whose dirty-faced kids are these?"

I quickly scanned the store to see if I knew anyone, ducking my head to hide from the judgmental stares of other shoppers. How many times had I been the accusing woman who mentally congratulated herself that *she* would never bring dirty children out in public?

―⁂―

One afternoon as my friends and I were watching our children at the park, the conversation turned to "lessons." Piano lessons. Dance lessons. Art lessons. Foreign language lessons. Swimming lessons. There were so many choices.

"So, Christine, what lessons do you want *your* kids to take? What do you want them to learn most?"

"Compassion," I answered. "It covers everything else."

―⁂―

Restoring The Joy

Compassion is more than sympathy. While sympathy comes from the Greek word "to feel," compassion comes from the Latin word "to bear." There is a big difference between "feeling with" someone who is in trouble and "bearing with" someone who needs help. Compassion requires action... action that can be observed... action that can be taught. Compassion includes sympathy, but it is much more. It's a desire to alleviate someone else's suffering.

For nine years during summers and Christmas holidays I worked for my father. No, I worked *with* my father. I was his dental assistant and office secretary. But I also discovered who my father was, besides being the man who was my dad. I watched him in his intense desire to do the best work for every patient. I watched his skill in turning a diseased mouth into a bright smile. I also observed the times he sat with a troubled patient to comfort and offer his help, even when his schedule was overflowing. He took emergencies in the middle of the night and on his days off. He took people who couldn't pay and gave them dignity... accepting whatever they could offer or working out an exchange of services or goods. He could, and he did. He taught me compassion.

―⚘―

Time and again my Heavenly Father showed His compassion to the people of Israel. They continued to wander from Him, falling away from His guidance. Each time He felt their suffering and renewed them, restored them. He could, and He did.

Time and again Jesus followed His Father's example and had compassion on those who needed His help. He healed their diseases and their afflictions. He fed them both physically and spiritually. He continued to do His Father's work. He could and He did.

―⚘―

Bearing one another's burdens shows compassion. Doing so without judgment is often a struggle. Too often I think that if *I* can do something... give up a bad habit, lose weight, resist a temptation, follow through with a commitment... then anyone should be able to do the same... all the time... in every circumstance... even when they are tired or in a hurry. No dirty faced kids! Ever!

Thank goodness the Lord has sent me more than my share of reminders over the years that just as I seek compassion, I should give it as willingly and generously... without adding to someone's load of guilt... without adding to their already heavy burden.

Jesus doesn't add to my burden of guilt. Instead He walks alongside me and carries that overwhelming burden for me... the burden He already carried to the cross... the guilt I can't always let go of.

And sometimes He carries me too... in His loving arms that never grow weary of showing me compassion.

He can... and He always does.

What Do You Want from Me?

"I can't let you do that," his wife said to me.

My husband and I were getting ready to leave Chattanooga after our vicarage year. We wanted to help the new vicar get settled by showing him and his wife around the city and helping them find a place to live. They reluctantly accepted the tour but balked at the offer of help in finding an apartment. I assured her that *we* had received help in getting settled in. She would love the generous, caring people in the congregation, who were eager to welcome the two of them.

"Oh, I won't ever let them help me. I wouldn't want to be beholden to them."

What? Did I hear her right? But, no, her husband echoed those same sentiments. These words sounded strange coming from a Christian couple, especially one preparing for the ministry. If this was their attitude towards the congregation, what did they feel about God and His blessings? I thought to myself, "This is going to be an interesting year for them."

The viewpoint of this young couple really isn't so rare in our world. There are people who are always looking for something in return. "What's in it for me?" Then there are those who mistrust our motives. "What will *you* want in return?"

Restoring The Joy

So many gods that people choose to follow are those who exact a payment. If you do enough good, if you are good enough, then good things will happen. If you sacrifice enough, if you follow rules and traditions, you should expect a return for your efforts. If that doesn't happen, then it must be your fault for not doing enough. How sad.

In Vanuatu, a nation of islands in the South Pacific, "What do I get in return?" is a way of life for some tribes. Friends who were Bible translators on one island found no word in the local indigenous language for "grace." Everyone was expected to return favors and "be beholden." Finally after many months of frustration, the death of one of the villagers provided our friends with the answer. What was done for the widow was not expected to be repaid. The word for this gift became "grace" in the translated Scriptures, and everyone understood.

A high school friend, a friend who had gone through confirmation and should have understood grace, once shared with me her concept of God. To her He was like the Great Accountant in the sky who watched her every move and kept a ledger of right and wrong. How sad I was. And I told her so, as I shared as best I could God's unconditional love for her.

What *does* God expect from me? Am I beholden to Him? Is that the relationship He wants with me?

When I was a teenager I received a call from our church's youth group president who wondered why I hadn't been coming to their meetings. As a typically busy teen I wasn't active in the youth group, but I had been involved with the music and Sunday school. I listened as she grilled me on what I had done for the Lord. I found myself defending my actions with a list of activities. But she persisted.

"What have you done *lately*?"

I finally told her it was none of her business. It was between God and me. And then I hung up!

I knew then and I know now... there is no way to pay God back for all He has done. Psalm 116 asks, "What shall I render unto the LORD for all

Leaving My Guilt at the Cross

his benefits toward me?" (v.12 NAS) Andrae Crouch's song "My Tribute" repeats the thought: "How can I say thanks for the things You have done for me, things so undeserved, yet You give to prove Your love for me?"

When Jesus walked this earth there was a woman who washed His feet with her tears. She wanted to thank Him for forgiving her sinful life.

We don't have our Lord with us to tell Him in person, to show Him our love. How *can* I say thanks? He gives me the answer in Matthew 25:40: "Truly I tell you, whatever you did for one of the least of these brothers and sisters of mine, you did for me."

In Arkansas a dear retired friend helped me in countless ways with my young children. She and her husband were the "go-to neighbor" if I needed someone to watch my little ones or to rescue me from a household disaster.

I said to her one day, "Marie, there is no way I can ever repay you and Frank for all you have done for me." Calmly she told me that there was never a thought in her mind for any kind of payment. She said she knew the day would come when I would pass on the kindness and love she had shown me.

Ah, the "pass it on" kind of love. And yes, over the years the Lord has given me a multitude of opportunities to do just that.

And yet, it's nice to be appreciated. It's nice to be thanked... even to be noticed. How discouraging it is to come home and not be acknowledged by the family who are in the house but are busy with their own activities. When the dog is the best greeter, something's missing.

I wonder if God feels that way about me sometimes. His creation... the sun, moon, stars, wind, flowers, trees... greets Him, acknowledges Him 24-7. Yet I'm sometimes so busy with my own life I don't always take the time to let Him know I care that He's even there. And I'm the most important part of His creation... the one He died for!

I know I can't ever pay Him back for all His blessings... but I can use my life to say thank you.

Just greeting Him every morning... yes, maybe with a formal prayer... but also with my whole heart singing Rosemary Hoover's song, "Good Morning!"

"I love you, and I thank You, for living in me just one more day!"

Now that's a great place to start!

Coals of Kindness

"Oh, cookies! Thank you!"

I put the plate on my kitchen table next to the growing array of goodies neighbors had been dropping off all morning. We had just moved into the neighborhood with our three young children. This was really a friendly welcome. But when the next woman rang my doorbell with a loaf of bread, my curiosity begged an answer.

"Do you welcome *all* new people this way?"

"Well... No... I guess I might as well tell you. Your neighbor next door found out you and your family had bought the Carter's house, and he started a petition to keep you out of the neighborhood."

"Why?" I wondered out loud.

"Because you had children and a dog. There are no other young families on this street and very few in the subdivision. The rest of us were so mad at him that we didn't want you to think we shared his attitude."

I couldn't believe what I was hearing. He didn't even *know* us. He didn't like us because of who we were? My children weren't wild. They were cute and well behaved. I thought so... and so did most people.

I soon found out my new neighbor would be a constant worry with his unreasonable reactions to our living next door. I had to decide quickly what my response would be. The children were watching, after all.

I continued to greet him as if we were friends. I chose to be as pleasant as possible in apologizing for things I knew were unfair criticisms. I

Restoring The Joy

refused to give him a reason not to like us. And over the next five years I taught the children to do the same.

Meanwhile he and his wife lost out on the friendship of our three little ones. Others on the street became surrogate grandparents, bringing gifts of handmade toys and dolls, preparing special bags of goodies for them at Halloween, waving and smiling as the children rode by on their trikes and bikes. The neighbor next door continued to erect barriers, physical and personal.

"You can pick your friends, but you can't pick your relatives." My mother used to quote that old saying. It really doesn't go far enough. You also can't pick your neighbors, your coworkers, the person who sits next to you in class. The Lord puts us up close and personal to many people we wouldn't have chosen. Some of them are real stinkers! How we react is a major test of faith at times. People are watching how we handle the person, the situation, ourselves. It's a tremendous responsibility to be His witness at these times.

I wish I could say I have always made the right choice, said the right thing. I can try to explain away my less-than-Christ-like responses by claiming exhaustion, frustration. It's the last straw! (That's always a good excuse.) I try to justify my bad behavior. But I always suffer consequences when I do. It's hard to rebuild relationships.

The "coals of kindness" (see Prov. 25:21-22) that I heaped on my neighbor did win him over. Just a few months before we moved to California, he called to me across the chain link fence.

"I want to apologize," he said. "You and your family have never given me a reason to think unkindly of you. I was so worried when you moved in because my wife's health is frail and she didn't need anything to upset her. You have been really good neighbors, your children are wonderful, and I'm sorry we haven't been closer."

Leaving My Guilt at the Cross

He wasn't making excuses. He just was explaining. I assured him with a smile that I welcomed his words.

Unfortunately there are situations that cannot be resolved... no matter what we do. A few years ago I did strike out with words, words I don't regret to this day. It was righteous indignation at harm caused to my family and friends. This couple wouldn't have recognized any attempts to be kind.

My daughter came running into the house that day in tears. Our neighbors had just accosted with vile language one of our dearest friends who had made the grave error of parking in front of their house... on the public street. For several months this had been an ongoing issue with various people in the neighborhood who dared to even park *across* the street from their place. When I found them sitting in their own parked car next to the curb, guarding their territory, I lost it.

"What's wrong with you people?" I asked. "You don't have to have a reason to be nice!" I shouted as I turned my back and walked away.

After that especially unpleasant afternoon, my husband and I chose to ignore rather than continue to confront these neighbors. Those were the last words I spoke to them. I didn't like what I was hearing in my voice. And I didn't want them to change me into the very person I was objecting to. It was time to turn it over to the Lord. For the next ten years, until they finally moved away, my stomach no longer wrenched every time I saw them. I felt much calmer knowing He was taking care of it.

It's wonderful when we can say to someone, "I'll take care of it." Relief is in their eyes as the burden of fighting a losing battle is lifted. I know how light hearted I feel when my husband or a trusted boss speaks those words to me.

Restoring The Joy

And I know how grateful I am... when I struggle to make sense of the world my Lord has placed me in... when I fail to live up to His expectations... to hear Him say, "Don't worry. I'll take care of it."

He has done just that... and He always will.

Who Died and Left You in Charge?

There goes another one! Goodness, this is a mess! First my husband decorating the pink bathroom with spaghetti. Next Carrie Anne sitting up in bed and covering her blankets and sheets with a variety of dinner selections. Finally Jacob... standing and whimpering in his crib... covered in crud. Thank goodness number three wasn't due for another four months.

"Mom! Where are you?" I cried.

Oh... that's right. *I'm* the mom.

—∞—

"Who died and left you in charge?" was a saying we used to toss at each other when we were young. Usually it was because we were bristling at another's sense of responsibility.

But in many ways, every day each one of us is in charge of someone or something. We have responsibilities. We can't escape them. Not really. We shouldn't and usually we don't want to, except when they become overwhelming.

Responsibility sometimes is left to us by those who have gone before us... at work... at church... at home. We take up the challenge and the mantle (like Elisha) and move forward, hoping to do as good a job or better. If our parents made mistakes, we are not chained to their behavior. If a committee chairman or department director left too much undone, we have the chance to finish the job... and inspire the next person who comes along.

And the words I never like to hear when I'm in charge? "Wish things were like they were before."

Moses heard that lament from the Israelites on more than one occasion. His leadership was questioned. He was forced to listen as the people whined and complained and begged for their previous life, even if it meant slavery. Moses had finally gotten into the groove of leadership after a rocky start, first arguing with God about the wisdom in choosing him. Then going toe to toe with Pharaoh, honing his skills as the one who would lead the Jewish people from Egypt.

Now in the desert, following the cloud and pillar of fire from place to place, he was discouraged and complained to God about the people he was expected to lead: "What am I to do with these people?" (Ex. 17:4) and probably thinking... "this responsibility *You* gave me?"

John Wesley, a great man of faith, had a mother equal to his strength and determination. He was the youngest of fifteen surviving children. How many days she must have asked, "What am I to do with these children you gave me?"

She found her escape. Throwing her apron over her head, she went to the Lord in prayer. Her family knew not to disturb Mom or cause any catastrophe while she was consulting with her Boss. Yet each time the apron came down the children were still there. I'm guessing her attitude had changed though.

There is a difference in the way one expresses the phrase "I *have* to." There are endless piles of "have to's" that we cannot escape. However, when I remember that many of these responsibilities are truly blessings, I can change my tone... from one of whining... to one of "I can't

Leaving My Guilt at the Cross

help myself. I just *have* to!" And then the joy returns, the excitement in seeing what new adventure this responsibility will bring.

Thank goodness the Lord sends me people, just as he sent Moses, to help me meet my responsibilities. Friends, coworkers, family, loved ones. It's my responsibility, but I don't have to do it alone. And of course I can always depend on my Boss to give me the courage, the renewed spirit to carry on.

As great as prayer is, as much as I enjoy my conversations with my Lord, the apron comes down. Like Moses I'm encouraged, no *challenged*, by God to get off my knees and get moving! (See Ex. 14:15-16) I have work to do and it goes beyond the everyday. There is more to my responsibility than just my daily chores.

Who left me in charge? My Savior Jesus. He not only died, but rose, and ascended and entrusted me with the marvelous challenge, responsibility, privilege, and joy of taking His message of salvation to a world that so desperately needs it.

It's a daunting task. Certainly the handful of followers who heard that first command to "Go and make disciples of all nations" (Matt. 28:19) must have wondered "Really? Just us?" But look where His message has spread and is continuing to spread because of all of the blessings of communication and transportation!

What am I to say? I really have no other option if I truly love my Lord. How can I say no to the one who willingly gave Himself totally for me, who didn't shirk *His* responsibility.

Those disciples have died long ago as have others in the years since. Now I'm the one, not necessarily in charge, but charged with the task, the *joy*, of sharing His love.

And My Lord promises He is with me… and all those who follow after me… "to the close of the age."

Can I Help You?

"This shoe is amazing! I can't remember the last time I put on a new shoe and didn't feel my feet complain one bit."

The helpful gal in the shoe department told me they were the Nike Free Training shoes. They were designed to conform to my feet. *My feet?* The ones with all the funky little bumps and flat arches? The ones that demand to see at least ten pairs before they are remotely satisfied... and maybe not even then will they let me take the shoe home to break it in? But now I felt the shoes and I were one, and my feet were left speechless. Time to head home with my new walking friends.

—⚏—

It's important to replace things that are no longer serving their purpose. My old walking shoes were providing little support. Some old comforts... shoes, slippers, toothbrushes (yes, toothbrushes)... can even become unhealthy. I have to remind myself to throw out my toothbrush when I know it must be harboring germs from my latest illness.

But when we start using the replacements, they don't feel quite the same. Shoes and slippers are snug. New toothbrushes just feel funny in my mouth. But that reminds me they are doing the job the old ones could no longer measure up to.

So what to do with the old? Shoes I've worn out really aren't safe for anyone else to wear. They might become my "garden" shoes. Old toothbrushes? How many should I really keep around for cleaning in tight places or around the sink faucet? Certainly I wouldn't dream of keeping old shoes or toothbrushes in the closet or cabinet with the new ones! I take stock of the space I have and start tossing.

Sometimes my habits are like my shoes. I've grown *so* comfortable with them. They are a big part of my day... my life. I know my life is full, and I have a limited number of hours in my day. And I have new, *good* habits I want to start including. Some of the old ones may not be really serving the purpose they used to. I keep doing them just *out* of habit. But others really are good for me. I *like* some of my old habits, and I want to keep them.

And then there are the others. Time wasters. Things that don't really support me and my relationship with others. Or my relationship with my Lord. I know it's time to take stock and start tossing, but I hate to give up some of those that have become such a part of me and my lifestyle.

New wine in old wineskins (Matt. 9:17). New beginnings in the company of old bad habits. Not good combinations.

Paul says we are a new creation in Christ (2 Cor. 5:17 ESV). I'm His child! I've been saved, once for all time! I've been marked as one redeemed by Christ the crucified! I've received His forgiveness!

But I seem to spend too much time fitting Him to me instead of me to Him. He promises that we will be a good fit together, just like my new Nikes, but I sometimes treat Him like those shoes that I need to break in. Why can't I just let Him comfortably clothe me in His righteousness, the perfect fit every time, instead of suggesting improvements and insisting on my own way, my own style, the "shoe" that causes all sorts of problems if I insist on wearing it?

Leaving My Guilt at the Cross

When I put my training shoes on each morning I am reminded that I need to work out, walk, anything that will help me improve my physical life. The wonderful fit encourages me to keep going.

My life with Christ is also a training session. The dictionary says that training means to direct the growth of... to teach... to prepare... to form by discipline. Oh... that last one is the hardest. That's the decision of what to throw out and what to keep.

Fortunately my Lord's promises are new every morning. He can't wait to "dress" me for the day. And I need to feel the wonderful fit that encourages me to keep going... to consciously enjoy the touch of His hands adjusting His robe on me.

Oh, right... the prayer thing...

When I can't decide what to toss and what to keep, when I feel discouraged with my bad choices, when I find myself resisting His direction... that's when I hear his voice.

"Can I help you?" He asks every morning... and all through the day... every day.

Left Behind

"So... who should I leave behind?" I asked my mom. She had assured me I was foolish to take all three of my little children out in a boat to go fishing. But each sweet face beamed its excitement for this adventure.

"Good question," she chuckled.

Poles in hand, life jackets snugly fastened, we hit the high seas! Okay, maybe we rowed just a few hundred feet from the lake's shore... but this was heady stuff for my young ones.

The fishing trip was a mixed success. The winch for the anchor rope was jammed, and the anchor never seemed to quite grab bottom... so we kept drifting. I spent most of my time and energy rowing back to the prime fishing spot, a collection of underwater boulders that was a perch and bass playground. At one point Jacob prayed fervently over a scrawny little fish I was working on that had swallowed a hook. However, in the end, three pan-sized fish were our trophies. The best part was we were in it together. No one was left out.

—⚅—

As much as we like to be independent thinkers and doers, most of us like being part of a group. The camaraderie, the shared interests give us an identity outside of just being ourselves. Even those who insist on maintaining their separateness can't avoid being labeled. They become part of the "free spirit" group.

Restoring The Joy

What I bristle about in the sociology of life isn't so much the group labels but the assumptions and even prejudices associated with them. During the years when I was mainly an "at home mom" we rarely "partied" with people outside the church. On the rare occasions when I found myself in a group of strangers, the response to my introduction pleasantries could be summed up with "Oh" as in, "Oh, you poor, unfortunate, unexciting, unfulfilled woman." I found the perfect solution. The newscasters had recently proclaimed that it took $250,000 to raise a child to the age of 21. From then on I introduced myself as the CEO of an independent consulting firm with assets close to a million dollars. That got their attention!

I think of my other labels, such as English teacher... everyone's favorite subject in school and a title sure to create uncomfortable conversations with people who are constantly self-checking their grammar. I've also had people "console" me on being a pastor's wife, "That's a *job* that must be the hardest one in the world!" Fortunately I've had the pleasure of correcting not people's grammar, but their impression of who I am according to the various labels I wear.

A few years ago I read Ruby K. Payne's book, *A Framework for Understanding Poverty*. She was adamant about the need for a positive identity, a healthy spiritual and emotional awareness, to break the cycle of poverty. She also insisted that strong role models were essential in creating this spiritual identity. Role models were "paramount to maintaining a lifestyle with some semblance of order" (p. 24).

Now some people like to make themselves their own role model. "I'm my own person. I just can get in touch with myself." Well, I know every time I try that route I come up empty and frustrated. I'm not a very good rock when it comes to emotional and spiritual stability. What's my measuring stick? My sounding board? My accountability?

Our Lord knew that spiritual poverty has nothing to do with social status or wealth. When He spoke of the "poor in spirit" He was looking over the crowd that had gathered and saw people who covered both genders and various ages and social positions. He promised them that the kingdom of heaven would be theirs.

Leaving My Guilt at the Cross

I like the New Living Translation that refers to the poor in spirit as "those who realize their need for Him" (Matt. 5:3). This is an all-inclusive label, a group that includes me. On top of that, Jesus promised to be the role model I can rely on, the one I can trust completely. The never changing, stable Rock.

There are those around us who also realize their need for Him or maybe are just realizing they have a need for something. Something that doesn't keep disappointing them. Something that gives them that stability to face each day. Even if they don't want to admit it, they are searching for a role model.

They are also searching to be part of something, someone. That's when I have to be sure I'm not standing in the way of their view to my Lord. I need to be that welcoming witness that wants to include others... that reaches out with His love. When someone who doesn't understand my close walk with my Savior says to me, "There's something different about you," I love it! Then I know my cross is showing even when I'm not wearing one.

The best part of being His child is that I know I have the Lord's identity, His label. He is always part of me. And I don't have to stand by and let people's prejudices and assumptions decide what "being His" means.

When He says, "Come to me all you who are weary and burdened" (Matt. 11:28) I know He always includes me in His promises.

He would never think of leaving me behind.

Remote Access

"Just click on the place where it says 'Allow' and I'll be able to figure out what's causing your problem."

Now this wasn't my computer friend Eric, whom I trust completely to not mess up my computer or access my personal information. This was a fellow half way around the world in India who wanted to take complete control. I knew my computer wasn't working right. I knew I couldn't fix it and certainly my husband couldn't either. Okay, *I* called *him*; *he* didn't call *me*. I knew the company was reliable.

"Click."

Who do we trust in this world? We trust the drivers on the road to stay on their side. We trust the doctor and the anesthetist when we have surgery or a procedure. We trust our dentist not to create an irreversible disaster in our mouths. We trust our barber or hair stylist to not create something we can't live with until it grows out.

Sometimes it seems we trust people more than we trust God. He knows this. He even gives us a laughable example of our misplaced trust. A loved one wouldn't give us a stone instead of bread or a snake instead of a fish (Matt. 7:9-10). If we trust a human to give us good things instead of bad, certainly we can trust Him. And yet we don't ask. We don't trust. It's as if we don't think He truly cares about us!

Sometimes I'm so busy with being who I am that I treat God as a remote access, just like the fellow in India. It's an emergency! I was just going along doing nothing out of the ordinary and suddenly I can't make it work! What's wrong? Help!

Then there are other times when I'm praying and praying and praying, looking for a sign from God, waiting for him to take control of the cursor in my life so I can just sit back and watch Him clean up my messes. But He isn't like the computer geek. He isn't going to let me just sit on the sidelines of my life. He isn't moving the cursor around without me. His access isn't remote.

Instead, when I can feel His hand on mine, I know my loving Savior is right there with me. I can trust Him to correct my path... watching Him turn my disappointments into blessings... helping me to click on the right icons in life so that I can live abundantly, just as He promised.

Initially I didn't call Him. I didn't know how to access Him or even that I needed Him. But in the relationship I have now, as one redeemed, I continue to strive for Him to be my constant companion. I know I can trust Him in all areas of my life... especially those that only He and I know about... my personal information.

And yet I still hesitate. I want complete control. I don't want His suggestions. I trust myself. I don't trust that He will only give me good things if I let Him.

In the midst of my resistance, when I close my ears to His voice, my Lord continues to encourage me to initiate the conversation.

And when I don't, He daily knocks on my door... asking me to open... helping me to grow in that intimate relationship of trust... inviting me to click on "Allow" so He can have access with His power to heal and strengthen... today and every day.

It's in the Bag!

"No, you can *not* take your clown into church!"

Noah's sad little face melted my determination to be firm.

"Okay. But you have to keep it in the bag. If you take it out, Mommy will take it away."

Amazingly the little guy, only two and a half years old, sat quietly in the pew next to me, listening to the service. His little hands firmly clasped the top of the closed bag on his lap. Every few minutes he carefully unrolled the top and peeked down at his clown and then just as carefully rerolled the bag.

No one knew us at this church. We were on vacation and had chosen a service that was starting just as we pulled into Nashville. But our children were used to being in church. Noah, the youngest, was completely aware of what was going on, taking it all in, participating in his own way. At the same time he was totally aware of what was in his bag and how precious it was to him.

Noah never disturbed the woman sitting on his other side, but I knew she couldn't help noticing his bag... or his constant checking... calmly reassuring himself that his precious clown was still there... and then returning to the service.

—⁂—

I like to think that I'm always keeping God close by, close at hand. I know that hasn't always been true. Sometimes we're tempted to leave

Him behind... thinking we won't have as much fun... worried that if we're not careful, people will notice He's there.

Over the years I've learned that when I do take God along, my life is better, my choices are better. It's not like He doesn't want me to enjoy life. I've just discovered that His idea of fun is much fuller and more lasting than what the world sometimes has to offer.

And I also have found out that it's okay when people notice we're together. I hope they feel I'm checking on His presence in my life. I hope my conversations and comments are "God inclusive"... letting others know He is precious to me without hitting them over the head with my "bag" to get their attention.

—⚜—

After the service, the woman sitting next to Noah turned to me and kindly complimented us on our children's behavior in church. But what she *really* wanted to know was, "WHAT IS IN THAT BAG?" She said she just *had* to know what could keep a little fellow so quietly attentive for such a long time.

That's what I want people to ask me. What keeps you focused? Why do you have such assurance in life? Why are you able to weather the stuff life throws at you? How can you stay calm in the midst of tragedy?

The Lord knows my gift isn't overt evangelism. I can't go up to random people on the street or knock on doors. But He knows I can share what's in my bag. He reminds me that I can be prepared to give an answer when people want to know the reason for my hope (1 Pet. 3:15).

That's the greatest part of sharing... letting people know what God means when He says to us, "It's in the bag." It means to be certain, assured, guaranteed. It means that it has been achieved, completed, secured, accomplished, won. Heaven is ours!

Now I'm not in heaven yet, but I know heaven is my true home. I'm just enjoying His heavenly promises in a temporary location, knowing He is with me every step of the way.

My Savior assured me of all of this when He proclaimed, "It is finished!" That was His guarantee that I never have to worry. It's in the bag!

You'll Get Used to It!

Balancing on five-inch stiletto heels, I felt the siren scream of pain shooting up the back of my legs.

"These are all the rage for gals your age," the young salesman assured me.

I was in my mid twenties, and since that time I have seen this particular fashion craze come and go at least three more times. I couldn't believe the pain, and I told him so.

"Oh, you just have to get used to it!" he said.

Stories of foot binding in China flashed through my brain.

"No, I don't!" I handed him the shoes and walked away.

—⚭—

Over the years there were many things I had to get used to because the end result was something worth the discomfort or even pain. Orthodontics and retainers. Contact lenses (the hard ones you had to adjust to). The dizzy feeling of bifocals. Sore muscles from exercising. All were worth it because I could look down the path and see that light of accomplishment or relief.

Then there were (and unfortunately still are) other times when people like that shoe salesman encouraged me to take paths I knew were not right. And I allowed myself to take those paths, dark ones, assuring myself it was okay, hearing a voice say, "You'll get used to it." And at times I did.

One path I found myself on wasn't exactly dark, but it was dim enough, and it was leading me the wrong way. I was in my mid forties, that comfortable age when the body is letting you know that life isn't going to exactly spring back to the "before picture" with ease. I looked in my closet and found exactly two skirts and one pair of pants that fit.

"That's okay," I thought. "I'll just throw on a variety of scarves and no one will notice I'm wearing the same thing every day. The elastic waistbands are so comforting, and besides, I'm not ever going to look twenty something again!"

It's so easy to continue down paths, even those we fool ourselves into thinking are well lit. Our eyes become accustomed to the dark. We can become accustomed to the darkness in our lives... get comfortable in it. Enjoying the elastic waistband that keeps expanding to accommodate our poor choices. Throwing on a scarf in an attempt to hide the truth that our present path really has no good options.

Just as the darkest desert sky brings out the light of the stars, sometimes it takes a really dark, even bitter, part of our lives to see the stars God sends us... a scripture, a song, a person, a closet full of unwearable clothes, a doctor's report. Sometimes the reminder is gentle. Sometimes it's a whack upside our conscience.

He knows me. He knows what I need and when. He knows what will get my attention.

Then comes the recognition.

"What am I doing to myself? My friends? My family? This isn't me! This isn't who I am!"

When the darkness overwhelms me and the light around me becomes night, He reminds me that darkness is not dark to Him, and the night is as bright as the day (Ps. 139:11-12 NAS).

He says to me, "You are right! This isn't who you are. Not only did I make you, but I purchased you, won you, redeemed you. You *are* better than this. You are a new creation!"

In the dark I hear His voice and see His light.

"Trust in Me. Look to Me and My light."

And the more I do, daily seeking His lighted path, the brighter are my days… and the more I get used to it!

You're Not the Boss of Me!

"So... are you going to sort through the things in that cabinet?"

"Yes."

"Are you going to move everything out of that corner and sweep it?"

"Yes."

My husband pointedly answered all my questions and then turned to me.

"You asked me to clean out the garage. Are you going to let me do it, or do you want to do it yourself?"

Oh. I guess I'd better just close the door and get busy on something else.

—⚏—

It's hard to hand over responsibility, even to people you know can handle it. I ask someone to stir a sauce on the stove, and then find myself lifting the lid to give it one more round for good measure. When the children were learning to take on chores around the house, I had to figure out how to teach "attention to details" without discouraging them with too many suggestions.

The hardest thing to hand over was leaving our children alone for an evening without a babysitter. They were certainly old enough to be on their own, but the struggle for authority amongst them was not productive. We decided that each would be responsible for his or her own behavior. No one was the boss. However, they were all responsible for each other's safety and could step in if anyone was making a dangerous choice. That seemed to work. We never asked too many questions as long as the house was quiet upon our return home.

Most of us resist micromanaging. We don't work well with someone constantly looking over our shoulder, commenting, suggesting, criticizing. We like the freedom of doing it our way, especially if we think we have better ideas.

Herman Melville in his book *Moby Dick* has a lengthy discussion on what some call "the fabric of life." If you can imagine a loom with the vertical threads in place, that's called the warp. It doesn't change. It is predetermined. Then there is the woof. It's the thread attached to the shuttle that can create patterns at will. In fact, this sums up Melville's thoughts on man's existence. What he refers to as necessity, fate, or destiny is the unchanging part of our lives, the warp. We, however, have a free will that moves the woof threads through life making things happen for good or evil. Then there is the unexpected accident of something hitting the fabric as it is woven... chance... which he claims is impulsive and indifferent, and is the final determiner of the outcome of one's life.

Now this is a neat little package that to me looks like an attempt to explain responsibility. I'm just glad that I can include my Lord in this picture, or I would definitely be depressed.

I know that God knows how long I will live and what my future holds. That's because He's already in tomorrow and the next day and the next year. But that doesn't mean my fabric is already laid out for me to sit back and enjoy.

Interwoven into my daily life with all of its responsibilities and challenges and joys is my real job, my real purpose in life... bringing His message of grace and love to others, wherever I meet them, however I'm involved. He has the perfect message. And who does He trust it to? His imperfect messenger... me!

Leaving My Guilt at the Cross

Thankfully my Lord doesn't micromanage me. He gives me the opportunity to try new ways to touch people's lives. He rejoices in my adventures and discoveries. He loves it when I include Him in my choices and decisions. He is always there and knows just when to get involved.

And I am constantly amazed at His better solutions, ones that I would never think of myself. That's part of the "chance" that Melville talks about. But note, it's only part of it.

There is also someone... sometimes myself, sometimes someone else, sometimes the devil... who deliberately or carelessly throws a disaster into the mix. Or something just happens because of the condition of this world... sickness, accidents, forces of nature. Then how quick I am to say, "Why could you let this happen, Lord?" How honest I should be to say, "Why didn't I check with you first?" or "Why did I think I had all the answers?" or "Why should I be the one who is spared?"

With humble heart I need to turn to His guidance. With eyes of opportunity I need to look for the way He's going to bless my disaster or the unexpected tragedy that hits me between the eyes.

Each day I make my plans, my list of things I want to accomplish. I have learned not to let it become my "warp" that doesn't change, the list I need to honor at all costs.

In prayer, I ask the Lord to guide the woof I hold in my hand. He has promised in Jeremiah 29:11 that He will prosper me, not harm me. He will give me hope and a future. When I don't struggle against His loving touch, I am ready for the unexpected sorrows *and* joys.

I say to Him each morning, "You know what I'd like to accomplish today. But I return this day as a gift to You... as You have given it to me, so I return it to You... to use to *Your* glory, not mine."

Pity Pots

Oh, no. There she goes again. No matter what the discussion topic, she manages to bring it back to herself and her woes. This is supposed to be a renewal time for pastors' wives, not an endless litany of our problems! We all have our issues. After ten years in the parish, I could certainly add my share. This gal had been a pastor's wife for only a year.

"Get a life!" I thought.

Finally the wife of a retired pastor, a veteran of years in the church, in her lilting Southern voice said, "Honey, I think we have all had enough. It's time you got off your pity pot and moved on." And thankfully that was the end of it!

God gives us a great "pity pot" story in the Bible. Although the book is called *Ruth*, it is really more about Naomi and how God turned her life around. Actually Ruth always did seem to have her act together. Maybe that's why I relate to Naomi better.

From the beginning, Naomi isn't a very positive person. (Notice she names her two sons "Sickness" and "Wasting Away.") And when things really go south and she is left alone with her two daughters-in-law, she drags herself back to Bethlehem... determined to shout out her spite and anger to all... asking those who greet her to call her Mara, the bitter one. Well, I know I would have been the last in line to ask that woman to my home to have a fun chat!

Now I like to think of myself as a generally upbeat person. I'm not a Pollyanna by any means, and I will shed the sympathizing tear at the drop of a hat. On the other hand, I usually have a positive approach to life.

There have been times, though, when I knew something wasn't right. My smile was forced. I couldn't bring myself to "give it my best" if I had wanted to. Darkness seemed to close in. I knew I needed help... from God... from those He sent me... my own "Ruth." Someone who cared. Someone in the midst of his or her own troubles who could encourage me.

And there were unpleasant situations, unfair trials, discouraging attacks that seemed to dominate my life... my conversations... my energy. That's when I would get a firmer "Ruth"... the one with the Southern lilt to his or her voice. The one God was speaking through to steer me back gently... and sometimes not so gently. Reminding me to lift my eyes. Get busy! Stop looking inward! Enough talk about that!

The "Serenity Prayer" by Reinhold Niebuhr encourages us to accept with calmness the things we can't change. It also asks for courage to change things that we can. Finally it hopes for wisdom to tell the difference. It's the wisdom I need the most.

I don't need to waste His precious gift of time or energy struggling with or pushing against something immovable. Putting on a brave face to the world as I melt down inwardly is exhausting. At the same time, I don't want to become bitter.

I have taken on a motto in recent years that helps me deal with those difficult times... those things that aren't fair... things that threaten to turn me into bitterness: "Blessings from Disappointments!" When, instead of wallowing in my self-pity, I look for the blessing that God promises He will provide, I can accept more graciously the downturns in life because I am already moving on. He reassures me with *His* serenity, *His* wisdom.

And He assures me that "*All* things work together for good to those who love God" (Rom. 8:28 NKJV).

That keeps me off my pity pot!

Listening for the Applause

We held our breath. Higher and higher they built the structure. More and more items were thrown up to the young Chinese acrobat until he finally flipped a cup to land on the saucer. I couldn't believe anyone could manage all of that *and* keep his balance on top of a precarious stack of chairs and tables. We applauded and cheered. He took his bow and left the stage.

Our visit to China several years ago included this wonderful performance in Beijing of talented young people. Not only were they masters at balancing, but their bodies bent in any number of positions. Incredible flexibility! How do they do it? Then again, how do *we* do it?

Balancing acts are not really that uncommon. We all perform ours to various degrees every day. Not only are we trying to keep ourselves in balance, but we are also balancing various tasks using different parts of our body and mind. Those tasks are familiar... family, work, friends, hobbies, children, church, classes. Where do they come from? Some, such as family and children are blessings from God. Others, such as work, are part of living on this earth.

Then there are those I choose to take on. Or sometimes other people throw new tasks and responsibilities at me. And just like the rings and balls that are tossed at the acrobat, they slide onto my arms and into my hands. I accept them and readjust. But then sometimes, like the acrobat, I gesture to someone to toss me one more into the mix. I can handle it! Really! Or can I?

I know that when I am busy I seem to accomplish more. At least that's the excuse I tell myself. After all, I'm a "completion type" person. Sometimes I relish the adrenaline that pumps through me in the excitement of getting so much done. You can only imagine the rush I get when I can check off a multitude of things from my "to do" list!

So what's the point of doing so many things? Sometimes it's to help others... a noble calling! Sometimes it's to give myself a feeling of accomplishment beyond the daily routine of chores. Not a bad thing either. But no matter what the justification, I get myself into trouble when I don't check in with God before I commit to one more thing. He reminds me to "count the cost" before I take on a project. He tells me it's the key to my balancing act.

But there is another part of the performance I need to guard against. Like the acrobat, I enjoy the compliments from others, their amazement at what I am able to accomplish. I listen as people say, "I don't know how you do *all* that you do!" Prideful? Yes. I smile... but then I have to admit when I look in the mirror, "I don't know how she does it either."

And then I hear that old saying about pride... and here comes the fall, the crash. I throw up my hands in frustration as if I had no part in it! God promised to not give me more than I can handle. Right? Oh... that's right... some of this didn't come from Him.

The saddest part of the Beijing show was hearing our son Noah tell stories about the lives of the acrobats we were watching. He said this was their whole life, their whole sense of accomplishment, their whole identity. Many had started as children and worked their way to this pinnacle of success. When someone did make a mistake, and we saw only one or two during the entire performance, it was sometimes catastrophic, not only for the act itself, but for that person's future. There was often loss of position in the company. In the Chinese community there was something even worse... loss of face for both the acrobat and the family.

Leaving My Guilt at the Cross

Thank goodness when I crash it isn't the end of the world by any measure. The Lord Jesus once again reminds me that when I am balancing on Him... not on my own strength... not on any "earthly prop that gives way"... I can handle more. He reminds me that when I foolishly... for whatever reason, but especially for prideful reasons... listen to others and assume more than I can handle, He is there to put it all in perspective. Once more He forgives me for my failure to lean on Him... *and* my failure to check with Him first.

The most important thing, however, is the applause. Right? Job well done! Keep it up! Thomas Wolfe in his book *Look Homeward Angel* talks about the "desire in the human spirit that seek[s] public gratification by virtuous pretension." Ah... craving the applause of the crowd! Assuming the spotlight that is really not mine. Self glorification... the greatest human flaw.

This is when I truly need to humble myself... on my knees... before His throne of mercy... asking for the courage to continue living my balancing act to *His* glory as a thank you for all *He* has blessed me with. Gratefully adding my applause to the sounds of creation... praising Him and Him alone.

Runoff

"Do we have a new pond in the back yard? Was that part of the new landscaping we just paid for?"

I assured my husband he didn't need to invest in any goldfish... and that I would take care of it... I hoped.

After a few days of unfruitful negotiations with our landscaping contractor, I figured out the problem myself. Thank goodness! We didn't need to drown our new, expensive plants or waste the irrigation water. The clay base under the topsoil was causing the water in another area to run downhill. Just readjust the timing on the sprinklers to find the right balance in order to maximize the absorption. Success!

Hmmmmm... the right balance to maximize absorption.

Now I'm thinking about all of those TV commercials that come on usually during the dinner hour when people may be watching and eating. You know... the ones that discuss the finer points of digestion and elimination. Of course we know the balance our bodies need, but we don't always eat to be sure we are absorbing our minerals and vitamins so they aren't just drained out of our systems. As I am "moving along in years," my body is more and more vocal about the lack of balance in the foods I put into my mouth.

Even if I choose good foods, sometimes I gulp or wash the meal down... in a hurry to get to something else on my list for that day. Supposedly my brain doesn't even know I am eating or getting full until twenty minutes into my meal. Yet I keep shoving it in past the point of what I really need! Where is the tasting? Where is the savoring? Where's the enjoyment?

Even worse is when I watch my family plow through a meal that I spent half the day preparing. And then they devour a pie (that took me hours to make) in five minutes or less! I know they enjoy it and the compliments are profuse, but again I ask... Did they even have time to taste it? Where is the savoring? Will their bodies even have time to absorb any of it?

Absorption.

When we begin our day, the hours ahead are already filled with work, errands, attending to children, attending to parents, appointments, and on and on and on. These are the "meals" of our living. As my attention gets yanked in various directions, I know I'm not the only one who sometimes is riding the "runoff" into the storm drain at the end of the day.

This is when I have to remind myself that the days of my life are not to be gulped or washed down. Instead, I need to take time to absorb what life is giving to me... what *The Lord* is giving me... wherever I am placed... whomever I rub up against. Remembering to live life before it's gone in five minutes or less.

Yet, there is no way I can absorb *everything... every day*. It's too overwhelming!

Absorption.

I sit down to the table of God's Word too. And when I gulp down the Lord's words with a quick read through, where is the tasting? Where is the savoring? I read scripture or hear it read in church. The Lord chooses just the right words to reach *my* heart, just for *me*... and I breeze through them in five minutes or less! I know I can't be the only one sometimes living on spiritual "fast food."

But in my busyness He reminds me that He is still feeding me.

"O taste and see that the Lord is good!" (Ps. 34:8 NAS) Now I remember He is there in each hour, each moment. His Word calls me to the feast. He doesn't limit the menu. He has prepared my meals for all eternity. He always has a "special" and it doesn't cost a penny. He feeds my mind and heart with words of comfort and encouragement... and forgiveness.

He asks one thing from me in all of this... to be sure I take the time for my soul to taste and absorb Him. Then am I truly strengthened. Then am I truly full. Then am I truly satisfied.

He helps me focus on what I really need to absorb... and tells me to let the rest go!

Lessons from Milton

"I was wondering. I'm sure the Hershey Museum focuses on his career and life, but does it include much on his philanthropy work too?"

"No, it doesn't," the young man at the information booth said. "But there's a lot on the schools and hospitals he built."

Suppressing a giggle, I gave him my best "nonjudgmental" smile and purchased our tickets.

Hershey, Pennsylvania, is just what you would expect. Chocolate. Chocolate. Chocolate. The street lamp covers alternate between giant wrapped and unwrapped Kisses. Even the main street, Chocolate Avenue, is paved brown as if you were driving on fudge. I'm sure the amusement park and the factory simulation tour with its singing cows would make Milton Hershey and his wife smile. But it was the story that captured our hearts as we wandered the museum. For a man who had only a fourth grade education, he was a great teacher... and still is.

Lesson One: Use only the best.

Milton Hershey used only the best ingredients, including fresh milk from local dairies. My mother somehow knew this about the Hershey bar in 1955. She said it was the best milk chocolate and the only candy bar she would buy for my sister and me.

Lesson Two: Design good things to be shared... and then share them!

The five-cent bar my mother bought for us was neatly divided into sections, perfect for sharing equally. One bar made two little girls very happy. If it wasn't too hot we could savor each little piece, seeing who could make her half last longer. I remember the first time Mom bought me a whole bar for myself. I couldn't believe the treasure! But I just had to give her part of it. It was too good to keep it all for myself.

Lesson Three: Don't dwell on what you don't have.

Milton Hershey didn't have much of a formal education, but he never stopped learning... from what he observed... from his workers who had inventive solutions to his manufacturing problems. He and his wife Catherine weren't able to have children, so they "adopted" hundreds of orphaned boys through their school. The Hersheys kept a close watch over those youngsters and often invited them to their home.

Lesson Four: Live and give so good things will continue.

Milton and Catherine didn't live extravagantly. They invested their wealth in the community and in the lives of their employees. They gave money to schools and churches. They built parks and hospitals. Milton knew that most wealthy men's good works died when they did, so many years before he left this earth he gave his company as a trust to his school for boys. His legacy of reaching out to orphaned and neglected children continues to this day.

I am most impressed with Milton and Catherine's attitude towards their blessings. They could have enclosed themselves in their wealth, comfortable in their success. But I'm sure they were no strangers to our Lord's words: "Give, and it will be given to you. A good measure, pressed down, shaken together and running over, will be poured into your lap. For with the measure you use, it will be measured to you" (Luke 6:38).

I don't think Milton Hershey worried much about his personal legacy. He was most concerned that people would continue to be blessed by what he had accomplished... by how *he* had been blessed.

So I've been thinking... What will be *my* legacy? Should I even be concerned with my legacy? I'm not a wealthy industrialist. I don't have enough money to set up a foundation.

Leaving My Guilt at the Cross

But I do have wealth... a wealth far beyond the world's small view. And I have a foundation, not established by me but for me. It included only the best... God's Son. His love is designed to be shared, not enjoyed just by me or a select few. The things I don't have pale in comparison to His wonderful gift of faith. And I can live and give without holding back because His fountain of grace never stops flowing.

And my personal legacy? As long as I keep my eyes on my Lord, He will bless whatever I do.

What really matters is building on His foundation. Touching as many lives as possible with the love of Jesus so they gain a closer walk with Him... a walk that will continue to touch others into the future... long after I'm gone.

There's a Word for It

"Mrs. Vogelsang, may I *please* go back to the classroom and get my toboggan?"

"I told you, George, there is not enough snow for a toboggan. And by the way, where *is* it in the room?"

"On the back shelf."

"Don't be silly, George. If there were a toboggan on the back shelf, I *know* I would have seen it!"

I finally gave in to his pleas, and moments later he returned to the playground.

"So where is your toboggan?"

"On my head!"

I chuckle to this day remembering all of the miscommunications I had with my students the year I taught in Chattanooga, Tennessee. The stocking cap confusion was just one laugh we shared. What we called things and how we pronounced words reminded me of a lesson I had learned in a college class years before: The word is not the thing!

Our trip to Quebec a few years ago was another reminder of words and confusion. My school French got us by most of the time, until we ran into dialect and vocabulary that didn't match the dictionary. Even when I had the right words, I didn't use them correctly at times. The gite (Bed & Breakfast) hostess gave me a cold shoulder when I commented repeatedly that the rooms she showed me were "tres cher." She warmed up quickly, however, when I caught my mistake. Instead of telling her they were "tres charmant" (very charming) I had said they were very expensive. Oops!

When English abandoned us completely in the far eastern reaches of the province, we both became stressed with the constant desire to be understood. One evening the menu was entirely in French. However, pictures accompanied most items. Thankfully we could just point. We didn't need words. We weren't going to starve!

Sometimes I am at a loss for words... when I'm talking, when I'm writing. If someone is generous, they might help me locate what I am searching for. I recite the alphabet in my head to remember people's names that escape me. A dictionary and thesaurus are my companions at the computer. Everyone needs help at times.

And then there are those who because of illness, injury, or surgery have lost cards out of their mental Rolodex. My dear sister-in-law became so frustrated with her inability to access words after her brain tumor was removed. I made light of the games we played searching for the elusive words. I told her that at least *she* had an excuse for not remembering.

Sometimes I am at a loss for words... when I have emotions to express to someone... my love, my joy, my sorrow. That's when I take forever searching the greeting card aisle for just the right sentiment... the one that captures my exact feelings. That's when, if I can reach them physically, I simply hold the person to me... letting my presence speak to them... giving them my heart and ears... to listen to them.

Sometimes I am at a loss for words... when I have emotions to express to God. My anger, my sorrow, my deepest grief. I cry out to the Lord... but with what? Gut wrenching sounds that make no sense. Hot tears that course down my face. I finally admit it.

"I don't know what to say! I don't know what to pray!"

When I say it out loud I can feel the strain start to melt away. "... the Spirit helps us in our weakness. We do not know what we ought to pray for, but the Spirit himself intercedes for us through wordless groans" (Rom. 8:26).

The Holy Spirit doesn't use words either? That's right. He doesn't need them. The Lord holds me, letting His presence speak to me...

giving me His heart and ears... to listen to me. And He doesn't wait to be asked. He's already there, waiting for me to notice.

When I acknowledge my weakness, that's when His power streams in. When I am weak, then He is strong. It is *His* strength that gets me through... conquers my sorrow, my grief, my fears.

There's a word for it.

Grace!

Tacking

Staring down the sailboat's almost vertical deck at the water rushing by, I clutched the tiller tightly to my chest as we carved through the waves. Perched almost directly above my instructor... leaning back against the gunwale with all my strength... I was certain that any moment we would be catapulted into the lake as the thirty-five-foot boat tipped over.

That calm, smiling man who obviously was enjoying himself (and thought I was too) finally zeroed in on my terror and shouted, "Push it away from you!"

What? Wouldn't that just make it worse?

"Trust me. Push it away!"

I had no choice but to obey... and then watch as the rest of the crew scrambled to bring the boat about. Oh... it worked.

—⚓—

"Please don't take the boat out without me," I told my older sister. "You don't know how to sail."

"Oh it can't be *that* hard," she said. "And besides it's just a little one-sail dinghy."

I couldn't claim our sailboat as mine, but *I* was the one who had taken lessons from the YMCA. She didn't have a clue.

Sure enough, when I got back to the cottage after work the boat was gone and so were my sister and cousin. From the end of the dock

Restoring The Joy

I scanned the water for the blue and white sail. Ah, there they were! I could tell the boat was moving closer... but no one was really sailing. Oh... someone was towing them back from the end of the lake.

Sailing is easy if you just let out the sail and go with the wind. Getting back home is another story.

Learning the art of tacking is the key to sailing. It allows one to get to any point desired, no matter what the direction of the wind. There's a sense of control, accomplishment. In my one-man boat I was responsible for everything... the tiller, the lines, the sail. I could go places, and I didn't need anyone's help.

—⚓—

Sometimes I feel like going with the wind, letting out the sail and watching life happen to me. It has its relaxing moments with little effort on my part. It's a great feeling not to struggle. But when complacency sets in, especially spiritual lethargy, I know it's time to return to my "home port"... the place where my true values are... the part of living that demands my attention and commitment. Then I'd better have the skills at hand, the lessons learned.

William Ernest Henley's poem "Invictus" ends with "I am the master of my fate; I am the captain of my soul." Alone on the lake with my sailing knowledge, it was easy for me to feel invincible. Even today when I depend on my own abilities and talents, I can convince myself I can do anything. After all, isn't that what the world tells me?

The Lord loves our ambition. It's His gift. So too are our dreams and hopes. They are His blessings that give life that glow. He loves when we become accomplished, using the talents and opportunities He has gifted us. But He also knows that we can't claim our boat... our life... as our own. My life *does* affect others. And others affect my life.

The majority of "Invictus" talks about prevailing whenever life challenges us or tries to overcome us. It's my nature to say I won't let something beat me. Prevailing is our God-given attitude... not just going with the wind... not giving in to terror. To be strong. To endure. No matter what... I must prevail!

Leaving My Guilt at the Cross

Of course then I can't be unsure... scared... lonely... or tired.

When I admit I can't do it... when my instincts fail me and I don't know which way to push the tiller... when the wind picks up... a really strong one... and I'm at the end of the lake heading for home, tacking for all I'm worth, praying a gust doesn't tip the balance, realizing I don't have all the answers...

Then I feel His hand over mine. I don't have to wait for Him to sense my fear. He knows.

I'm glad I'm not alone. I'm glad I can hear a voice that calmly slices through my terror:

"Trust me.... I have your heart... I have your soul."

I Need a Job!

My usually upbeat, cheerful Noah was in tears. We were in the midst of Saturday chores and he had been helping me fold clothes, something he was really good at.

"Carrie has the bathrooms and Jacob gets to vacuum and dust. I don't have a job," my nine-year-old wailed.

I assured him he was a great help to me, but he insisted he didn't want to just help. He wanted something of his own.

Later that day his dad and I took him aside and offered him our proposal. I would teach him to sort and wash the clothes. Everyone's clothes. He was ecstatic! He quickly learned to use the washer and dryer and soon was taking us to task about unemptied pockets. Years later he would be the one to show his brother and sister the fine points of laundry when they went off to college.

—⚘—

In his book *Haiti After the Earthquake,* Paul Farmer recounts the emotions of the people who were devastated by two hurricanes and a massive earthquake. Over and over their cry was, "Don't do it for us. Use us to do it. Give us the training and opportunity." This was especially true of the farmers who couldn't understand why food was brought in from other countries when they could sell their own produce to the agencies for distribution. They didn't want handouts. They wanted jobs.

Sometimes we aren't helping people by doing things for them. It takes away dignity, pride, ownership, purpose.

For fourteen years I took my fourth graders to a senior day care center near our school. I always stressed that as we worked together on various projects it was so important to not do it *for* their senior friends. Have the patience to let them work through physical difficulties. Discover how much they could do and the skills they had.

My favorite visit was when we made salad and cornbread as part of an evening meal for Interfaith, the local sponsor of meals for those in need. This was a task these older people knew how to tackle, especially the ladies who hadn't been given an opportunity lately to use their kitchen skills. Each year Gloria looked forward to stirring the cornbread, especially when I told her the first time that she was an expert. She was useful, she had purpose, she had pride. Not the puffed up pride the Scriptures warn us against. Pride in a job well done.

I think of the excitement of the disciples, first the twelve and then the seventy others, who were finally sent out by our Lord. Getting to use their training. Telling others what they had seen and done with the Christ. Coming back and sharing their stories among themselves and with Jesus. They had purpose. They had pride.

I have pride in jobs well done... a clean garage, a neat garden, a spotless car, a tidy house. It's a great sense of accomplishment to see purpose, to be useful. But it isn't long before those things need attention again. Thankfully I don't have three little ones behind me anymore... undoing everything I've straightened up.

But I don't live in a museum. Things, tasks, jobs of this world are often never ending. And yet they sometimes seem to be the ones I focus on... the ones that get most of my time and energy.

The Lord understands that at times I am harassed and can feel helpless. The last thing I need is another job. But that's exactly what He has for me. In addition to the daily tasks of living I have a job that, if I do it right, renews my energy instead of draining me.

My Jesus says to me, "The harvest truly is plentiful but the laborers are few" (Matt. 9:37 NKJV). Now I'm not a professional evangelist. I'm not a person who can knock on strangers' doors. But the passage says laborers. Not CEOs or managers but common, everyday people without specialized training, given a job that anyone can do. He isn't going to do it for us. He wants us to have ownership, purpose in His kingdom. He knows it's what I need.

Actually I realize I am doing this job every day, whether I'm aware of it or not. What I say and do is part of my "job" when it comes to witnessing to who I am. Sometimes I'm not very good at it. What I say and do doesn't bring joy to others or to my Lord.

Other times I don't shift my focus away from things that could be gone tomorrow and towards things that matter for all time.

Or else I act like the disciples who stared into the sky as Jesus ascended... waiting to be told to move on. Waiting for my faith to be realized in His promises and forgetting to extend that hope to others. Keeping my understanding of His joys as some kind of secret.

I *am* just a common laborer in His field. But I know I am useful. I know I can live my life so others will want to know my secret. And then I can share my story, my life of freedom.

So what do you want me to do, Lord? I need a job today. I want to feel the excitement, the eagerness, the pride in knowing I have *Your* message, not mine, to share.

So just show me where.... and I'll be on my way.

How Do I Love Thee?

Oh no... He's not there! He must have become really seasick. Poor baby.

I'd been enjoying our trip out to the island bird sanctuary from my spot at the boat railing. The waves and wakes were rocking our path, but I was hoping my husband's SeaBands would keep this from being a total disaster for him. Now he had disappeared from where I had left him on an inside bench... directly across from the bathroom. The beauty of the rocks and birds drew me back to the view, but I kept glancing over my shoulder every few minutes.

He's missing it all! But he really loves me to weather this agony so I can experience this new adventure.

As we rounded the island heading for the dock thirty minutes later, who should appear at my side but my husband. Not at all green around the gills but chatting about the trip out that he had enjoyed... from a great spot near the front of the boat... just out of my view.

Elizabeth Barrett Browning in one of her most famous sonnets tells her husband, "How do I love thee? Let me count the ways." She really goes on to talk about how *much* she loves him, not exactly the *way* she does. There's no discussion whether she sews on loose buttons or makes him his favorite dessert. She doesn't say anything about writing him notes of encouragement or laughing at his jokes. Instead she speaks of her devotion, that ardent, eager affection and support she gives to him. There is never a question that her love for him exists.

A flurry of conversation recently surrounded the book *The Five Love Languages* by Gary Chapman. In it the author encourages people to discover how the other person in their relationship wants to be loved, cared about ... and then satisfy them with those various desires. While this is a wonderful idea, I'm not sure it's the best.

My husband has a long history of showing his love. Many of them revolved around my father's testing of his character and his commitment to me: "Certainly you would love to sit in a darkened hallway and see my endless slides of the national parks... So glad you are chopping that wood for the fires we'll be enjoying six months from now, when you aren't here... This is the way to clean creosote out of the woodstove pipe... Just place that load of patio blocks in a nice pattern under those picnic tables over there... We need to get the insulation under the house before the winter sets in, so you need to go down into that crawl space..." (And my favorite for my perennially seasick husband)... "I'll be getting you up about 4:00 so we can get out on the lake before sunup. The fish should be biting just about then."

Now these weren't the romantic demonstrations of love most would expect. They weren't really very personal. No backrubs. No flowers. Just pleasing my father and showing his devotion to me. I've learned over the years that recognizing *how* someone loves me or cares about me is more important than sitting around waiting to be "loved" according to my preference. I can hire someone to give me a massage. I hint at lots of people that I love to get flowers. I don't need the one who is devoted to me to do those things.

It is a question of knowing. It is a question of appreciating someone for whatever gesture they use to show their devotion. Thanking them. Returning their love.

God knows how I really need to be loved even when my constantly changing list of demands and complaints shows that I am never satisfied. Sometimes I'm like that petulant child who opens all the wonderful Christmas gifts and then wails that the one she had her heart set on isn't there.

"He forgives all my sins and heals all my diseases. He redeems me from death and crowns me with love and tender mercies. He fills my life with good things" (Ps. 103:3-5 NLT).

And yet I complain, "If you loved me you wouldn't let this happen. If you loved me you *would* let this happen. If you loved the world so much, why do these sad things continue to happen?"

My insistence on God proving His love is little more than waving my arms in front of Him to get His attention. "Do what I want! Show me you love me!"

There is no question that God loves me. As John says in his First Epistle, "God *is* love" (4:8). He *is* devoted to me. That ardent, eager affection and support is just for me.

He did love the world so much, He does love *me* so much, that He gave me what I really needed... His ultimate demonstration of His love and devotion... His best... His one and only Son... in my place... for my failings.

And I know He will accept whatever I do to show my love. He enjoys however I return my love to Him... as long as it is sincere... as long as it is my best... as long as it comes from a devoted heart.

Now What?

What do you mean turn right? That would take us to Riverside and we need to go to San Diego! At least this time she knew we were in California and not parked in front of a house in Ohio where we had left her in limbo on vacation. I was finally tired of arguing with our GPS system ("Gar-*mean*-a") and turned her off. Fortunately my cell phone app made more sense and we arrived at our friend's house without further confusion.

Having a general idea which direction we are supposed to be heading is very helpful. But when we are in unfamiliar territory we tend to rely on directions from others whether they come from a real person or a handheld device. I get really nervous watching a spinning screen that hunts frantically for my location... or staring at the "searching for satellites" message that never resolves. Locals who don't really know names of streets but rely on gas stations and McDonald's for landmarks can be frustrating. Usually we arrive at our destination with a smile, but other times we are definitely headed for a dead end.

When we are taking unfamiliar paths, whose guidance do we trust? Sometimes it's helpful to listen to those who have been there before or who are actually on that path. After all, experience is a wonderful plus. But can we always trust them?

I remember a faculty I once joined who was at odds with the administration and, in addition, was divided against itself with a number of factions. Early on, each group took me into their confidence and warned me about the others. I decided not to align with anyone but take the "high road" and just be friends with all. But that only earned me suspicions from just about everyone as to my true motives. There apparently wasn't a right path, just a dead end.

Directions can lead to positive encounters... and others that can seem more like a collision course. At times we are the ones making those directional changes, and we have our path laid out just so. Other times we feel like we are being shoved or maybe even dragged down a path that seems not only unfamiliar but scary.

Though there are people (ourselves included) and events in this world that may think they are determining our course, it's really the Lord who ultimately is our guide.

When my children feel overwhelmed facing uncertain times I remind them that the Lord says He is a lamp to our feet and a light to our path (Ps. 119:105). I tell them that God is not going to give them a searchlight down the road into the future. He is lighting each of our steps, so that when we follow His light directly in front of us... by reading His word, praying, and listening to His voice through His messengers in our midst... we will not stumble or be led astray or fall off the path.

That verse from the Psalmist also says the light is unto *my* path. It is a personal path... just for me. It also is the path that I have... whether I like it or not. Maybe it's a path I have chosen to take. Maybe it's an adventure that I'm not quite sure of.

And maybe it's that path I feel I am being pulled down or pushed along. The Lord knows about that path too. "Yea though I walk through the valley of the shadow of death..." (Ps. 23:4 KJV). That path through danger and the threat of death isn't one that the Lord creates for me. That's the one the world would throw me down. Then His light to my path is crucial. "I will fear no evil, for Thou art with me" (ibid.).

Then again, maybe it's a path that *is* divinely inspired. Okay, I'm not a famous evangelist like the apostle Paul or Billy Graham, but I'm still divinely inspired. I just need to remember that I am in partnership with *His* plan, not the other way around. I need to resist the temptation to say, "Here's my plan, Lord. Do you think you can help me out here? Here's the address. Here's where I want to go."

And if I'm thrown off His path or wander off on my own? If my direction changes and I sense a dead end? Then I feel His hands brushing me off, turning me around, planting my feet firmly back on His path. I am repositioned. I have my bearings... His compass... His direction.

I don't know what the future will open to me. But when I think about it, I have to ask myself how important *is* it for me to know what's next? I doubt the caterpillar knew it would one day be a butterfly. And If I'm honest with myself, I have to admit I don't really think I could handle that searchlight down the path.

But when I search with His light, checking His word, tuning in to His voice... then I know I have a clear connection that I can trust on my path... in my life.

Pace Yourself!

I was starting to see stars, but I had only a few more feet of the flowerbed to clean out and then I'd be done. I hate not finishing!

Moments later, sick to my stomach, I staggered into the coolness of the house and collapsed face up on the carpet. I had pushed the limit once too many times. Fortunately my husband (who had been repeatedly calling me in from the heat) brought me water to drink and a cool cloth for the back of my neck.

"You shouldn't push yourself like that. You aren't up to that pace anymore!"

A restaurant where we recently ate had a special promotion for a series of menu changes they were having over the next two months. They encouraged us to pace ourselves so that we would save an evening every two weeks to savor a new experience. They wanted us to enjoy the variety and also to not overdo any one thing so we would keep coming back.

When our son Jacob was in fourth grade he qualified for a long distance, city-wide race. The "Turkey Trot" took place on a day I couldn't attend, but I heard the story... how he burst from the starting line with the other top runners. Unfortunately when the lead group appeared from behind a building, Jacob was no longer with them. He'd spent it all and dragged the rest of the way to the finish line. However, he soon learned, thanks to a great career playing soccer, to mix bursts of speed with endurance running.

Sometimes illness or an injured body forces pacing on us either as a temporary visit to the bench or as a permanent readjustment. After her bout with polio my mother found she could no longer dance or bowl like she used to. I didn't have the joy of watching her skip through life. But I never remember her sitting on the sidelines completely.

From the viewpoint of a little child I would often ask my mother why she was relaxing on certain days. She would tell me that she had worked hard the day before and now was taking it easy. I'm learning to take that advice from her book of wisdom.

When we are young the possibilities seem endless... along with our energy and abilities. I remember thinking I wanted to read everything and learn everything... a goal that obviously had no finish line but still was tempting.

In my midyears I found myself juggling dreams and possibilities, usually taking on too much and sometimes having no view of a finish line in any direction.

I was told on my 60th birthday that I was an official grownup. I'm seeing the advantage of this. Looking through a wide-angle lens I seem to have a better perspective of time and space. Patterns and rhythms are falling into place. Certainly I have regrets of things I've done or left undone, but I now can place them in the forgiving, loving hands of my Lord Jesus.

Then again I also find myself getting a little panicky when I realize that the years ahead are fewer than those behind me. How many more sunsets? How many more times will I see those leaves change color? How many more Christmases with my family? Fearing the passing of time the temptation is to cram as much as possible into each day, each hour, each minute. I'd better get this in. I want to do this before I'm too old or sick to enjoy it.

There's the other side of this too. When I'm in the midst of what to me is one of those treasured moments, I want everyone to stop and also enjoy it, to savor it, to be able to keep coming back to the memory. I sometimes overdo it, however, and force everyone to stop for *my* memory... insisting they drop whatever they are doing or absorbed in to join me. That can be annoying and frustrating to my family.

I love the picture of a young child with her hand in the gentle clasp of an aged grandparent. They enjoy the same pace in life... one because of her youthful, undeveloped abilities... one because of the limits of age. One taking time to dream and explore... aspiring, wondering what is to come. The other, whose dreams are memories, also wondering what is to come.

I also love God's pacing. In creation he set the pattern, the pace. He could have done it all in an instant, but He set the pace for us, including a day of rest, not for His own relaxation, but because He knew His creation needed it. He knew *we* did. Can you imagine no night and day? Can you imagine no day of rest?

As a Christian my day of rest is Sunday, the first day of the week. I like that because it reminds me I'm not collapsing into the pew after an exhausting week, but instead starting my week with the renewal that comes from pacing myself to absorb His nourishment. Getting my pacing right for the week ahead so I'm not gasping from one thing to the next... so I'm not frantic in my enjoyment of life.

When I ignore this pattern... His pacing... I know I suffer physically, emotionally... and spiritually.

And that's when my Lord is ready with His cool cloth of forgiveness.

Falling

I looked up at the Montreal Hospital sign above me as I lay sprawled on the sidewalk. Well, at least I chose a good place to trip and fall on my hip. Gingerly picking myself up, praying the vitamin D and calcium I take had worked their strengthening power, I assured my husband that I was good to go. Our vacation wasn't ruined. That night I found only a small bruise on my hip. To my dismay, over the next two days it grew into a purple burrito-sized tortilla!

There are lots of fears about falling. Babies exhibit a startle reflex because of it. My fear of heights is really a fear of falling... a long way down. Older people (Oh, that's me now!) are worried about how a fall could change their lives completely.

Some falling we look forward to. Falling asleep after a struggle to turn off a racing mind. Falling into place or falling in line when things have been in a state of confusion. Falling in love when we discover that friend is becoming someone to share more with.

Other falling isn't as defined. Someone claims to have "fallen upon a great idea," as if they had no concept of what goes into inspiration. When something "falls somewhere between one thing and another," we are critical of a lack of certainty. However when the tests come back and our numbers "fall within the normal range," we breathe a sigh of relief.

As parents we dread hearing about some falls: "Your child is falling behind." And we will do anything and everything to fix that fall.

Most falls we try to avoid. We fall down. We fall off, over, into, beneath objects. Teeth and hair fall out. We fall out of favor with friends and bosses. Objects, sometimes really big objects, fall from the sky. We don't like it when things, including our emotions, fall apart. Falling for something, we vow never to be taken in again!

But then there are those falls that we allow to happen... or that seem to be out of our control. We fall away from someone or something... or into darkness... into a hole... into a rut. We use the word fall because it helps to excuse our behavior. It wasn't my fault. It was an accident. I tripped. It came out of nowhere. I was pushed.

Really? Did the fall cause my problem, or did my problem cause the fall? Like Adam and Eve I am quick to justify my fall as if the fruit of disobedience was shoved into my mouth.

Yet there are truly those times when the fall is out of our control for whatever reason. Panic sets in and makes the fears even worse. Times when my life seems to be falling apart make it difficult for me to see God's hand and His plan.

In my free fall, it's easy to become selfish. What's going to happen to me? Why did this happen to me? Am I never going to get out of this hole, this rut?

That's when the Lord reminds me to take my inward focus and cast my eyes about me. "Check out how others are doing," He urges me. "Do not merely look out for your own personal interests, but also for the interests of others" (Phil. 2:4 NAS).

His strength returns me to my feet, still bruised, but ready to be used to encourage someone else. It's amazing how I feel Him working through my words and arms when I reach out to others who are falling... who have fallen.

He also reminds me to take stock of *my* fall. How much was my own fault? What can I do to guard against it happening again?

Just like my husband's voice, I hear Him saying, "Look down at the sidewalk to see where you're going! Remember to pick up your feet and plant them firmly on the path!"

But then the overconfidence returns, my self-assurance increases, memories of the fall slip back into a corner of my mind. And I am primed for a repeat performance.

Leaving My Guilt at the Cross

That's when I need to fall before my Lord... asking for His guidance... His forgiveness for not trusting Him... and His assurance that He is there to catch me!

I Don't Know My Own Strength!

Just a nudge with my hip and the piano will be lined up so I can see the director. Before I could do anything to stop it, the big studio Wurlitzer began its fall to the high school choir room floor. Mesmerized by what was coming their way, the front row of the bass section watched as it crashed inches away from their feet. Keys popped up and I was sure I had destroyed the sounding board. How could I, barely 100 pounds, have created this horrible scene?

Sometimes it's just leverage that tips a piano or gives the advantage to the weaker person. I still remember joking around with my then boyfriend, now husband, who outweighed me by more than fifty pounds and towered over me with his gangly frame. Before I knew it he was sprawled on the ground behind me. I never felt one bit of strain lifting him over my head.

Our physical strength is sometimes a mystery to us. Sometimes it's adrenaline that allows us to do heroic deeds. Sometimes it's shear will that gets us through sleepless nights with a new baby or to work on a project that has a demanding deadline.

Despite my stoic Norwegian heritage, emotional strength is not my gift. I come from a long line of criers on my mom's side. My Aunt Maybelle was the queen of fountains. She cried for every occasion... hellos, goodbyes... sad or joyful times. Her whole being trembled with emotion.

I'm not far behind. I cry at reunions of families even when I don't know any of them. I cry at commercials. During a movie or sermon that is touching everyone's heart my children are sure to lean forward to check out Mom to see if my eyes are welling up with tears. If they're not, that's all it takes to get me started. I tell anyone who is sad or grieving that I will gladly sorrow with them.

Yet there was a time early in our ministry when tears were not helpful. A man in our congregation had just found out that his missing wife had committed suicide. We received the call that the police had just found her body. Moments later our doorbell rang, and I welcomed in the grieving husband. He collapsed on my shoulder and we stood there holding one another. I didn't sob with him, though my heart ached for him. I felt a calm strength I had never known before. I looked at my husband and he just nodded.

Later I asked Bill what had happened. Why didn't I cry? Where did that strength come from? He told me the Lord was using me.

"Don't be surprised when it happens again. Get ready for more."

"Me? The weeping willow?" I thought. "That's not my strength. What are you thinking, Lord?"

Sounds a lot like Moses, doesn't it? "Me Lord? I'm not a great speaker. I can't lead these people. It's not my strength." Yet it wasn't long before Moses was confronting Pharaoh with bold confidence in the Power behind his words.

Later in the wilderness Moses had other strength issues. This time he just kept plodding along, not even realizing his energy was being sapped. It took a visit from his father-in-law, someone with fresh eyes, to take stock of the situation and give some very good advice.

"You will surely wear out, both yourself and these people who are with you, for the task is too heavy for you; you cannot do it alone" (Ex. 18:18 NAS).

Then he suggested Moses train others and delegate responsibility for some of the jobs.

"They will bear the burden with you... then you will be able to endure" (Ex. 18:22-23 NAS).

What a wonderful reminder that God puts me into a family and into a community of brothers and sisters in Christ for a reason!

Moses, however, had an ego that got him into trouble. When he struck the rock for water and it didn't flow immediately, he struck again in impatience, arrogance... forgetting where the power was really coming from.

When I start to take credit for God's power working through me, my strength begins to fail too. Things don't work like they did before. I have no leverage.

When I feel weak and powerless I don't like it. I keep striking at the rock... and nothing happens.

But when I finally admit I'm helpless... hopeless... then I begin to feel the Lord coursing through my body, my mind, my spirit. Strengthening my faith so that I am bold and confident once again.

The Lord promises in the Gospel of John that He lives *in* me and *with* me (14:17, 20, 23). He will continue to teach and remind me that His strength comes through His Spirit, through His Word... through others He sends to me, surrounds me with.

At the end of his life Moses reminded the Israelites how blessed they were, how great their God was.

"What other nation (people) is so great as to have their gods near them the way the Lord our God is near us whenever we pray to Him?" (Deut. 4:7)

What other person is so great, so strong, to have her god near her the way the Lord my God is near *me* whenever I pray to Him?

I *am* strong. I *do* know my own strength. It is nothing without Him.

It Must Be Nice

"I was wondering if you could watch our house and pick up our mail for a few days. My husband's parents are taking the whole family on a week's cruise to Alaska to celebrate their 50th wedding anniversary."

"Well," he drawled. "It must be nice."

What? Am I supposed to apologize for this wonderful opportunity? I gave some half-hearted justification of why it was going to be such a good time for us all, but finally I just stopped. Thankfully he is a great neighbor and agreed to keep an eye on things. But all I could think of was how he had deflated my party balloon.

"Gee, I'm so happy for me," I thought wistfully.

Sometimes good things *do* just happen to us. I think of Joseph who was the eleventh son in a family of twelve brothers but still was the favored one. Was it *his* fault that Dad loved him the most of all his children? Joseph didn't ask to be put in the back of the group with his mom for protection when his Uncle Esau could have wiped out the family. He also didn't seem to notice that His father treated his brothers as second-class children even though they were born first. Joseph obviously didn't recognize the jealousy and hatred coming from his brothers as he wore his beautiful, multicolored coat.

We sometimes find ourselves in a position similar to Joseph. Good things come our way because of God's blessings or because we are in the right place at the right time. As adults we usually can detect the jealousy of others, but sometimes we are blind to it or can't see through the facade others may be putting up to cover their envy.

But then there are things we really worked at... things we felt we deserved... and we bristle at the comment, "You're so lucky." Wait a minute. This wasn't just handed to me. I still had to work at it.

In his book *David Copperfield,* Charles Dickens talks about the combination of talent, opportunity, and hard work. He says talent and opportunity form the two sides of a ladder, but the rungs "must be made of stuff to stand wear and tear; and there is no substitute for thorough-going, ardent, and sincere earnestness."

Yes, I am expected to use the gifts God has given me and improve on them. He tells me that in the parable of the talents when the one person is chastised for simply burying what he has been given (Matt. 25: 24-28). We see this abandoning of talents all around us today. How many "gifted" musicians and athletes have gone nowhere? I know I need to guard against this lack of "sincere earnestness" when it comes to using what the Lord has blessed me with.

The ladder image goes only so far though. If I start to think that somehow I'm climbing a ladder with my rungs of earnest attempts to please God, I'm climbing to nowhere. I'm not even moving up. That's when Joseph's robe comes into view once again.

I have a robe too. My robe isn't multicolored, however. It's as white as the sunlight, whiter than any bleach can produce. But just like Joseph, I didn't earn it. I didn't even deserve it! It was given to me and I don't have to apologize or make excuses about having it.

The great thing about this gift is that it isn't exclusive to me. My Father doesn't play favorites. There are robes for everyone. There is no need for jealousy or envy. I'm so happy for me... and for you too!

I remember hearing the arguments from a young man who just couldn't accept the fact that he had a robe available... ready for the moment when he recognized he couldn't climb the ladder to perfection... ready for the instant he heard the Lord's voice calling to him... and felt the forgiving love of His Savior who had purchased that robe for him with His own life and now was robing him in His righteousness.

"So you're telling me it's *that* easy? God just forgives your sins because of Jesus and you can walk right into His holy presence?" I can almost hear his dismissive, disbelieving voice scornfully sniff, "It must be nice."

With a smile that doesn't condemn but earnestly desires understanding, I can only reply, "Oh, it is!"

You Make Me Feel So Young

"Oh, how funny! Those teenage boys are flirting with me!" As I headed towards the intersection, the two of them kept looking at me, waving and winking as their truck tried to keep pace with me in the traffic. At the light, finally reaching their goal, they pulled up next to my car and looked over... and down in astonishment... at my full, eight-month pregnant belly. With a smile and a wave, I tucked that little event away to remind me that at twenty-eight I was still young. Well, at least I felt that way.

Isn't it flattering to be thought of as younger than we are? Perhaps someone asks for my ID for proof of age (That doesn't happen much anymore!)... or flatters me by calling me "Miss." It's really a small thing, but it lifts my spirits for just a moment.

But just how far back do we want to go? No one likes to be called childish or be told to "Just grow up!" Childhood limits us in what we want to accomplish. There are just too many things we can't do because we aren't old enough.

Yet it might be nice to be a child once again... not have the responsibilities of an adult... to let someone else watch over me. And as I grew up there would be the chance to revisit some of my old mistakes... regrets... a chance to right some wrongs.

God talks about children a lot in the Bible. First of all He puts our relationship with Him in place. He is the Father, and we are the children. He knows what our nature is, and it isn't pretty. "Every inclination of the human heart is evil from childhood" (Gen. 8:21). Being a child doesn't immune us or excuse us from bad behavior.

At the same time He cherishes our faith as children, when we are connected to him through baptism and the scriptures that are taught to us.

And we are told to teach our children about this relationship. This is what draws me to teaching the youngest of His lambs, the babies and toddlers in our Sunday School. Jesus insisted the children *and babies* (Luke says this) be allowed to come to Him, so He could touch them, hold them, bless them. Children are included in His salvation plan from the Old Testament to the New. "Things revealed belong to us and to our children forever" (Deut. 29:29). Later those "things" were "hidden from the wise and learned and revealed to little children" (Matt. 11:25). Jesus reminds us that the greatest in His kingdom are those who are like little children.

All of this talks about the faith, trust, eyes, and heart of a child. But what about the times in the Bible when we are told that we shouldn't just be content with the spiritual diet of a child... that we need to have solid food? That reminds me to grow in my maturing faith, the faith that is called on to give a reason for the hope I have. I can't rely solely on my childhood lessons if I want to gain a greater understanding of my relationship with my Lord... and be a better witness to others!

Back and forth the argument goes in the epistles. First I'm criticized if I don't move on to solid food. Then I'm warned that I need to go back to the "milk" basics if I get too impressed with my own learning and knowledge and miss the simplicity of salvation. It's a balance that I need to pay attention to.

As I watch Christians who are much older than I am, I'm impressed by how the Lord draws them closer to Him as their days are numbered and heaven is close at hand. It's almost like He's bringing them back to His basics... the milk of their childhood faith.

One of my favorite stories was relayed to us about a dear sister in the faith who was close to death. Bedridden for weeks, she sat up, swung her legs around, and dangled her feet to the floor. Her children were alarmed and asked her where she thought she was going.

Leaving My Guilt at the Cross

"Heaven," she answered calmly.

When they assured her she couldn't get there by getting out of bed, she pointedly said, "How do *you* know?"

I know I need to renew that childlike trust as one who knows heaven is always a breath away no matter how old I am. I know I need to feel that direct connection to my Lord without the interference that comes from being an adult.

My first lullaby to my babies when we finally had our moments alone in the hospital was "Jesus Loves Me." I've added a new-old prayer to my morning as I begin the day with the assurance of my Savior's grace:

I know Jesus loves me. I belong to Him. I'm the weak one. He's the strong One. "Yes, Jesus loves me. The Bible tells me so."

Making Time For...

"**O**h look!"
Everyone rushed to the huge classroom windows to see what we had been waiting for. Pressed noses to the icy glass, eyes wide in wonder, we followed the first gentle stars of snow to the grass. Each one promised to stay for only a moment, but the sure sign of winter joys to come definitely captured our delight.

Our elementary teachers were wise enough to give us time to enjoy the first of many snowfalls of each winter season. They made time out of our busy school day for us to just soak in the newness. If they didn't, they knew that all they had prepared would come in a distant second to our desire to watch. I don't remember any of them ever saying, "Oh, come on now. You've all seen snow before." They always seemed to know when we had soaked in enough, however, and could be brought back to our lessons. Even so, our eyes would continue to drift to the outdoor scene unfolding.

Were these teachers making time? Of course not. No one makes time except God. What we really are doing when we make time for something is making choices on how we will use our time. I like to say I *spend* time. It reminds me of how valuable it is and that there is a limit to the bank account.

It seems to be okay with most people if they are just "killing time" as if time were an adversary. Maybe it is in some cases... when we are waiting for something important, or someone important. We need something to do to keep ourselves busy to make the interloper of minutes and hours disappear.

Now if someone says I'm "wasting time" I bristle. Then again I have often declared vehemently that something is a waste of *my* time. I had no control over it. It happened to me without my permission. But if I'm honest I must admit I do have control of much of my time. And how much is really wasted? Thrown away? Not valued?

Why do I do the things I do? I have wondered what exactly was the purpose of some of the things I found myself involved in. A class I took or really *had* to take to fulfill a requirement.

"When will I EVER use this in my life?"

A job I had for just a few months or a volunteer position I couldn't say no to.

"What a waste of my time! I'm not even using my training or education."

But with hindsight comes wisdom.

That's true if we are looking with the Lord's "opportunity eyes." How much of what I have done can really be considered a waste of my time? I know many things have prepared me for what I am doing today. What seemed like chance happenings were used by God to develop my gifts... connect me with His plan.

Or they helped me gain perspective. I know that my past waitressing jobs have taught me to be sympathetic towards an overworked server or a newbie who is learning how to juggle and multitask.

With wisdom comes insight.

Again... *if* we are looking with the Lord's "opportunity eyes"... the vision that cues us into recognizing why we are where we are, doing what we are doing.

There are drawbacks to this constant evaluation process, however. We hear the phrase "treasure each moment." Well, this doesn't give me permission to use a filter. Who knows how many mundane tasks I need to fulfill before I realize my goals... or should I say, *His* goals. There are some moments that I can truly let go of and not "treasure" and my life will be full enough.

Then again, how am I to know which things I am doing are the important ones that will have meaning down the road? I really can't constantly be weighing the importance of each thing I do, or I will definitely come to a standstill.

The other well-worn admonition to "live each day as if it were your last" exhausts me. There needs to be an ebb and flow to life or I'm not going to have the energy to continue. It *will* be my last day!

With insight comes contentment.

Now I need the Lord's "eyes of value." If I am giving God credit for His accomplishments… if I am trusting Him when life takes a down turn…. if I remember my life is in God's hands and so is my future… then I will give my best in whatever I do. I won't question its importance. I'll let God worry about how He will use what I'm doing. As long as it's my best effort, I know He will bless it.

With contentment comes anticipation.

What more will God do with my efforts? What more is in store for me? As I press my nose to the window that gives me the view to my life, I know God is giving me time… making time for me… to enjoy the wonder of it all. And in time, my tasks pull me away from the windowpane to where my days continue to unroll.

But I am secure knowing that with my Savior at my side, the time that I spend with Him will never be wasted.

No Questions Asked

"What are you doing here? You're not supposed to be home for another three weeks! Do they know you left? Do you have to go back?"

"Mom! Stop! It's okay!"

I stared at my daughter standing on our porch. Grinning next to her was her friend Debbie, her coconspirator who had picked her up from the airport.

"I'm done with my Peace Corps assignment. I told you a later date so I could surprise you! Are you going to let me in?"

—⚞—

Questions. Our lives are filled with questions. As a teacher I discovered that a big part of my job was learning to ask the right questions... and that there was no such thing as a "simple" question.

There are all levels of questions, some requiring a yes or no and others demanding explanations. Even the simple ones are not always black and white, whatever that means. Have you ever tried to buy white paint to touch up scuffmarks on the baseboards? Or tried to match a black jacket with a pair of black pants that weren't cut from the same fabric?

Children have great questions. And annoying ones too. The "Why's" from a toddler can wear down the most resilient parent. Knock Knock jokes are based on simple questions leading to silly punch lines. "Can we" questions need guarded or conditional answers or else we hear, "But you promised!"

Fourth graders have an abundance of faith questions. Usually I was able to give my students reassuring responses, but there were some that I put in the category of "Questions for Heaven." I wasn't going to make something up just because they trusted my answers.

Sometimes questions really don't matter, so why ask them? A man once approached me as I was filling up my tank and asked if he could have a gallon of the gas I was pumping. He had run out of gas and needed to get home. There he stood, neatly dressed in a work uniform, holding his red plastic container. Did I really need to grill him on where his car was, where his wallet was? Didn't he have a debit card, etc., etc.? The pump clicked off as my last prepaid penny of gas dripped from the nozzle, and he started to move away to ask someone else. I stopped him.

"Of course I can put in a few more dollars." The only question I needed to ask was, "Will that be enough?"

Sometimes questions stand in our way. The woman who kept asking me questions as we stood in the lobby of the hospital came close to delivering our third child herself right where I stood.

When we first moved to California and I still had an Arkansas license, a grocery store would not accept my check unless I first filled out a complete questionnaire and got clearance from the manager. I walked away from the groceries in the cart and drove to the next store where the cashier there promised to take my check and out-of-state ID, no questions asked.

Some questions have an agenda. One evening I was foolish enough to agree to a phone survey. After I gave what I felt were honest answers, my opinions on various topics, the woman began to readdress certain questions... the ones she didn't like the answers to.

"Now if I were to tell you... would you *still* vote yes on that issue?"

Enough questions. Click.

Jesus was good at questions too. The Gospels are full of them. Some are part of His teaching. They introduce parables or are part of His creative comparisons.

Others are meant to alleviate our doubts and worries.

Leaving My Guilt at the Cross

"Why are you so anxious?" "Why are you timid in your faith?" "Why do you doubt?" "I'm here, I'm in control. Trust me."

Still others are direct questions to those He encounters.

"Do you believe I can heal you?" "Who do people say I am?" "Who do *you* say I am?""

And my personal favorite, the one to that man at the Pool of Bethesda: "Do you wish to get well?" Now that seems like a strange question, one that it seems everyone would of course give a strong "Yes" to. But follow that story in John's Gospel to the end and you'll see why Jesus asked it (see John 5:1-15).

Jesus was asked many direct questions from those around Him: "How many times should I forgive someone?" "Who can be saved?" "How do I get eternal life?" "Are you the King of the Jews?" "Are you the Son of God?"

These He answered clearly and to the point. There was no hedging or circumventing the issue. He knew these were questions that needed forthright answers

Many of Jesus' answers to questions were questions themselves. Too often the religious leaders were trying to trap Him, and of course He knew it. They finally threw up their hands in frustration at one point and asked, "Who *are* you?"

Jesus simply replied, "I've already told you. Why don't you understand?"

Sometimes I long for this skill to know just what to say and when. But then again I know I will have the answers when I really need them (Luke 21:13-15).

The saddest question I'm sure Jesus heard was, "Don't you care?" Once it came from His disciples in the storm tossed boat. The other was part of Martha's plea to get Mary to help her. His answers were meant to put things in perspective, to point to what was most important in this world... our relationship with Him. How could He *not* care?

Satan is good at questions that are deliberately meant to cause me discomfort... doubt: "Are you *sure* He is who He says He is?" "Are you *sure* you don't have to earn His favor?" "What if it's all a big lie?" "Don't you wonder if this discipleship is really worth it?"

I'm shaken when I try with my own reason and strength to respond. However, when I review all of the questions and answers surrounding Jesus in The Gospels, especially in John's book, I am fortified with my answer, my defense... of my Lord... of my faith... of my assurance.

And when I am standing at the door to heaven (if there really *is* a door) and Jesus is standing next to me, having picked me up from wherever I shed my earthly life, that door will open to me.

Then He'll whisper in my ear, "Just like I promised. No questions asked."

Swerving

"Oh, shoot! This pen doesn't work. I need to write down the number of that CD track before I forget it. What a great song for the choir!"

As I fumbled with my purse to find another pen, I realized I wasn't driving very straight down the freeway. My eyes darted to the rearview mirror and froze on the highway patrol car directly behind me.

"Forget the song. Pay attention to the road! Don't let him think there is anything wrong!"

Like most people I claim to be a really good driver at all times, despite evidence to the contrary. Even if I'm not distracted I could be sleepy or thinking about something that keeps me from being the efficient driver I know I am. It scares me when I catch myself daydreaming and I don't even remember driving through a familiar neighborhood or section of the freeway.

But I try to avoid some of the more obvious distractions that would cause me to swerve. When I pull up next to drivers who are not exactly following a straight path, I find them talking on the phone, drinking coffee, putting on mascara, or eating an enormous sandwich. Once during rush hour I discovered a woman feeding a bottle to the infant in her lap!

It's bad enough to be following someone who is distracted like this, but it is nerve wracking to be a passenger in a car driven by a distracted person. One driver in our family loves to carry on a conversation... using both hands for emphasis... and looking me straight in the eye!

"Keep your eyes on the road, please!"

Anyone who has driven for a number of years can recall times when an accident didn't happen or the accident could have been much worse. A friend described a close call when she pulled into the middle turn lane on a wet, dark road. At the very same time a truck coming from the other direction also moved into the lane. Thankfully both drivers swerved in opposite directions.

One time a big table fell from a pickup truck ahead of me on the freeway. To my relief, a huge semi took the full force of the table before the debris reached my car.

Some of us can even remember a time when a sure collision seemed to pass right through the car. Certainly angels had grabbed the wheel from our frozen grasp.

I like to think I'm doing a pretty good job driving down my life's road. It's easy to pat myself on the back because I'm not like others who are so distracted by things I would never dream of doing. But I have my own set of distractions, ones I really don't like admitting to or ones I really don't want to let go of. I convince myself I am perfectly capable of handling it all.

Sometimes I have too many tasks vying for my attention. Sometimes there are enticements that I can't pull my eyes from. There have been times when I've been so tired that I forget which direction I'm even going. At other times I feel overwhelmed by all the options, all the detours I could take. My mother used to have a phrase, "You're running around like a chicken with its head chopped off." I never really thought much of those words until she actually described the gruesome scene to me, ending with the final collapse. Talk about swerving!

Sometimes I'm like Martha, who felt responsible for everything surrounding the visit of her honored Guest (Luke 10:38-42). I find myself distracted by the truly unimportant. Instead I need to focus on who my Lord is and why He cares so much for me. Fortunately God has a way of putting people in my rearview mirror to jolt me back to my task at hand... being His child... being His witness.

There are times when it's too late to swerve around an obstacle in my road. The impact seems imminent, and swerving could create an even bigger problem. That's when He sends a semi truck in front of me to lessen the blow. That's when I'm grateful for strong friends and family in the faith.

And then there are the times I know He just takes the wheel because there is no other way to avoid a catastrophe. And I let the tears of relief and gratitude flow.

My favorite picture is having my Lord always sitting next to me as I'm cruising down the road... laughing, enjoying conversations, keeping me company. It would be so wonderful to just concentrate on our relationship, soaking in the joy of being so close. That would be heaven!

But I'm not quite there yet. And I don't always remember He's by my side.

Yet I'm still moving down my route here on earth... the one He has mapped out for me... a map that's filled with promises to not harm but prosper me... one filled with a future of hope.

And thankfully I can hear His gentle voice reminding me to keep my hands on the wheel... and my eyes on the road.

None of Your Beeswax!

"So just how many children *are* you planning on having?" The head elder of our church stood there waiting for my answer. My husband had just announced we were having our third child in a span of four years, and the quiet but audible gasp from the congregation already had me on my guard. How does the Pastor's wife tell a leader of the church it was none of his business? (or "beeswax" as we used to say to one another as children) After all, he had six kids of his own!

Smiling sweetly I answered, "I didn't realize it was up for a vote."

Some things are really none of anyone's business. I was very careful to shield grades on papers when returning them to students. Ridicule comes no matter if it is an exceptionally poor or exceptionally fine grade.

My mother reminded us every election year that her vote was her own private information. She didn't have to share it with anyone. That's why it's called a secret ballot! I follow her example to this day.

Privacy issues are a real concern these days, especially with electronic record keeping. I remember getting into a heated argument with one caller who insisted on my mother's maiden name. I reminded him that *he* had called *me*, and I had no way of verifying who he said he was.

One nice practice I personally enjoy is asking waiting customers to stand behind the privacy line at the pharmacy. I remember in the "good old days" when the next person in line was breathing down my neck... literally. The current rules supposedly keep any personal conversations between the pharmacist and the customer out of hearing range. However, when the patient is slightly deaf, everyone in the store is party to the "privileged" information.

Then there are those who don't seem to mind sharing even their most personal information with me... even when I haven't asked. This happens to me a lot.

One evening I was waiting for my husband in the lobby of the theatre. I shared this comment with a docent who had asked if I was ready to be seated. Hearing the word "husband" she launched into what seemed her full marital history of marriages and divorces, several of each.

God doesn't really need to ask us questions to know what's going on in our lives. Psalm 139 is a wonderful reminder of the futility of trying to hide things from Him. Where can I go? What can I say? He is everywhere and knows things I'm going to say and do before I even think them up. This used to make some of my fourth graders uneasy. Instead of seeing it as a comfort, their guilty consciences considered it a threat to their privacy.

As a parent I have often asked, "What happened?" and received the answer, "Nothing." The evidence of a mishap or poor choice was obvious to the most casual observer, yet the guilty child didn't want to share. Supposedly it was none of my business.

This reminds me of stories from the Bible when our Heavenly Father got similar answers. Adam and Eve when they were hiding their shame. Cain who gave the "How should I know?" response when asked about his brother's whereabouts.

Sometimes it's obvious that God truly is the mind reader He claims to be. The embarrassed woman at the well in The Gospel of John, chapter 4, discovered Jesus knew about her present and past life. The Lord also questioned judgmental people who wouldn't dare share their condemning thoughts (See Luke 7:39). He truly does know our hearts.

Privacy is not a good thing when we are sick or hurt. There are questions that we must answer forthrightly or we won't get the correct diagnosis. Worse yet is the possibility of a medication or treatment that shouldn't be administered... if only the doctor knew our complete history... if only we had shared *everything*.

The Lord knows privacy is not a good thing when our souls are sick or hurting. Yet He urges us to step forward, away from others who might overhear, away from prying questions from condemning people, into a closet even, and let Him hear the entire story.

There is no reason for me to pretend nothing is wrong when the evidence is all over my life. There is no reason not to share it all. He knows it anyway. I'm the one who needs to be reminded of the truth... not Him.

He wants me to know, though, that I am alone with my Comforter... *not* my Judge. I can feel His forgiving arm around my shoulder. I hear his renewing, restoring words.

"Yes, I know it all... and I still love you!"

Thanks

"Why can't they have a drive-up window at the pharmacy so I don't have to drag my sick children into the store?"

After being up most of the night, I had just spent three hours at the pediatrician's office with two little children and a baby. I was tired and cranky as I backed through the door of the store, lugging the baby carrier and reminding the other two to stay close to Mommy. I didn't notice someone was holding the door open until I heard his voice behind me.

"Hmph! Do something nice for someone and don't even get a thank you."

Oh great. Just what I needed... getting called out on my manners in front of my children. The same children I had been teaching to be polite. "What do you say?" "Say thank you!"

I wasn't in the mood to be chided, but I hunted the man down in the store and apologized for being ungrateful. And then I thanked him. But it wasn't the same. I could tell. I'm sure I gave some excuse about being distracted and overwhelmed. He wasn't buying it. Of course I was hoping for an understanding, "It's okay." But he simply stared me down and gave me another "Hmph!"... a little louder this time. Was he really trying to make me feel bad? Well, he did.

—⁂—

"Thank you" is such a part of our culture. "Thank you" is one of the first phrases we learn when speaking a new language. We tell people

Restoring The Joy

"How can I say thank you?" or "How can I thank you enough?" when we are at a loss for words or can't begin to return a kind gesture.

Even the entertainment industry is full of thank you's. At awards ceremonies. After performances and concerts. Elvis Presley's "Thank you. Thank you very much." has become a classic phrase. Groucho Marx in *A Day at the Races* has a whole routine surrounding "Thank you."

One of my favorite opening hymn lines is from "My Tribute" by Andrae Crouch: "How can I say thanks...?" When I consider everything my Lord has done for me and given me, I *am* at a loss for words. And I know there is no way I can ever repay Him.

I have heard people say it isn't necessary to say thank you. Now I'm not talking about the response we sometimes get from people we thank. The "No need to thank me. It was nothing." Every language I have learned has this type of phrase to express humbleness from the giver.

No, the suggestion that no thanks is needed has come from a companion when someone is doing something kind for me... a waiter, a maid, a doorman, a servant. The person who comments has placed herself and me above the others. There's no need. It's their job. It's what they get paid for. They don't expect it. Ah... they don't expect it. That's when I love to say thank you. I love the look of surprise and the smile of pleasure... a gentle nod to let me know they enjoyed my appreciation.

One day while waiting for my husband to finish his visitations, I was browsing through one of those wellness magazines one finds in hospital lobbies. According to an article, saying thank you, being truly grateful, is good for us. It's not just a polite thing to do. It's also spiritually renewing. They said that the joyful feeling is proof that being thankful is a good thing.

There was more, however. The article went on to say that there is actual physical proof through research that being grateful may improve our health. It boosts our red blood cell production and the quality of those blood cells. Now that's something to take notice of! Being thankful is good for us on all levels!

I wish I could say I live a life of thankfulness all the time. I do try to remember to thank just about everybody I appreciate. And I do pay more attention when I go through doors!

But I know that the One who gives me my all is the one I too often forget to thank. I have all the right reasons and excuses... I'm too busy, too preoccupied, too distracted, too tired, or whatever... to notice what God does for me. Instead of using "How can I say thanks?" as a springboard to list all of the wonderful things He has done for me... undeserved... unappreciated... I sometimes just think, "O, He knows I'm thankful. I don't really have to express it."

That's when I think back to that magazine article. It's not about Him. It's about me. I *need* to say thank you. It's good for me.

And for the many times I didn't notice my Lord holding the door for me, making my life easier and more abundant, I can only say, "I'm sorry I didn't acknowledge Your help, Your loving kindness. I was wrong not to say thank you."

Thankfully His voice caresses my guilty heart. "Of course you were wrong, but I made it right. And it's never too late to say you're sorry... and to say thank you."

It All Blends Together

"So, Mom, if I stare at it and slowly walk backwards, will I be able to see the picture? Something like the Magic Eye books?"

I couldn't believe it. There was Jacob standing in the Washington National Art Gallery with his nose just inches away from one of Picasso's famous (and expensive) paintings. The key to appreciating this pointillism effect was to stand back from the painting until your eyes blended the color spots into a picture. Of course my family had to take this cultural experience and create some fun... at my expense, of course.

Blending is an important part of appreciating things in life. Coffees and wines have a special blend. When I'm baking bread or a cake I read the instructions to blend thoroughly. There's nothing worse than to bite into some pumpkin bread and hit a lump of baking soda!

I am constantly encouraging my choir to blend their voices. Sometimes one of the sections isn't blending. Other times one section is drowning out the others, and I have to warn them to back off. We even have warm up exercises to work on blending. The whole idea of choral music insists on blending so that one or two voices are not distinguishable from the group.

Vacations can be a nice blend of learning, history, relaxation, and fun. Then again, if there is too much of one thing, the days can just blend together. I remember our trip to Israel several years ago. After about the fourth site of ruins, the rocks and walls all became a blur. Some pictures in our collection have no titles because I couldn't remember their significance or even where they were taken.

Sometimes days and hours blend together. Perhaps because of illness or loneliness, one day seems to be just like all the others. Routine can do this too. We can forget what day it is... because it really doesn't matter.

When the children were young we spent most of our time together. These were the days before school and sports imposed their calendars on our lives. Even after all three got past the "baby stage" I realized how one day just melted into the next. Now of course we had Sundays to set the week off to a good start with church and Sunday School. And on Fridays their dad would take them all off to the grocery store to sing and dance down the aisles. That was always a joy to look forward to... their fun and my quiet time.

But the other days weren't anything special. Until I decided to make them so. We picked one day and made it "library day." Others turned into "park day" and "swimming pool day" if the weather was good. If not, it was "game day." When Carrie Anne started kindergarten, my neighbors made Thursdays special by watching the boys while I went to a "Mom's Day Out" at church.

As a wife and mother, Mary must have had those endless, blend-together days too. Certainly every day watching her child grow up (even if He was God's Son) couldn't have been a banner day.

Yet there were those days that were special. We know because she told Luke about them, and he shared them in his Gospel. Although it says only one time that she "treasured up all these things and pondered them in her heart" (Luke 2:19), she must have witnessed or been involved in several events that gave her pause. These are the stories that are included in the Bible... her strongest memories... the ones she thought about often, quietly, deeply. Reflecting. Revisiting. Wondering.

One meaning of pondering is "inconclusive thinking." Sometimes our reflections don't lead to a neat ending. Sometimes life hasn't played out to the final conclusion. Many things are "pending." But that doesn't stop us from thinking about them. Wondering. Marveling.

When I step back from my life, allowing all of the little things to blend together into something bigger, more meaningful, I realize I have more "inconclusive thinking" than answers on some days. I wonder what is to come for my life and the lives of my husband and children. I ponder over the things I have experienced... accomplished... and left undone. And they can blend together... or become a blur.

But then I "Ponder anew what the Almighty can do!" (from "Praise to the Lord, the Almighty") He gives everything a fuller range of importance far beyond the individual moments of my life with Him.

Each day I can think about all of the possibilities open to me. And then I need to allow the Lord to blend it all together... not with a "magic eye" but with His clear vision of how He will bring significance to everything.

The next line of that favorite hymn says, "If with His love He befriend thee!" Now that's something conclusive. What a friend He is! He was born, and He lived, died and rose again to life in order to bring my life into focus... with His forgiveness... His grace.... His love.

Watching
(An Advent Conversation)

"Why don't you go outside and watch for them?" My mother was tired of hearing me ask when my cousins would arrive.

Time to stare down the street... then up the street. Walk to the corner and back. Walk to the other corner and back. Count the lines in the sidewalk. Count the steps up to Grandpa's porch. And then down again. One more look up the street. I was sure I would wear out my eyes watching.

"Oh! There's an anthill in one of the cracks. They are all so busy every minute of the day. I wonder how far down their hole goes."

And while I'm watching ants... my favorite Iowa cousins spill out of the car and run laughing to greet me.

—⚭—

"Watched pots never boil" is an old saying. It seems to take forever for some things to happen or arrive. We seem to think looking *at* or *for* something will hurry it along.

Then there are other kinds of watching. I was asked countless times to watch my little brother. Now that was more than observing what he did. I was expected to keep him out of trouble, take care of him. Something like the "angels watching over me" in the old spiritual.

When I'm walking along an uneven sidewalk I'm sure to hear my husband say, "Watch yourself!" or "Watch your step!"

Restoring The Joy

When I wanted to teach my children a skill, I told them, "Watch me now."

We also expected them to behave. They learned at an early age that people were naturally going to be watching the pastor's children. It was just part of who they were, so get used to it.

"Watch out!" is a sure sign of danger. Be on your guard! Expect an attack!

Sometimes, though, we are just watching, just observing. Watching TV can be wonderfully passive when we want to relax our minds. However, when we hear someone "just stood by and watched" it usually means he *chose* not to become involved.

The old concept of "watching" was a real occupation. The watchman was paid to stay awake and look for anything that might be a threat to the community. Some buildings today have night security keeping watch. Sleeping during one's watch is a sure way to get fired. Be vigilant! Pay attention! I certainly don't want to be blamed for something dreadful happening "on my watch" no matter what time of day it is.

I also don't like to watch what I eat, especially during the holidays.

The worst watching, however, is when people are waiting for me to make a mistake. They listen to every word and take note of every thing I do, expecting a slip up. I mentally tiptoe around the room hoping to avoid hearing "Aha! I knew it!"

God watches me and He watches over me, takes care of me. He watches what I say and do, not to catch me doing wrong, and certainly not as a disinterested observer. He's just God. It's part of who He is. I'd just better get used to it.

And I've learned to watch *for* God. I give each day to Him and watch to see how He's going to use me, use the situations I find myself in, use the people around me... to work His plan for that day and to prepare me for the days and years ahead.

Down through history God's people have been watching. From the earliest times they watched for the coming Messiah. But like people who watch down the subway track, the trains that came along weren't the right one. The Messiah didn't come. And God's people kept watching for His sign, His signal.

And there was silence for four hundred years.

I wonder what God's faithful people were doing during that time? Wearing out their eyes watching? Getting distracted? Keeping busy doing mindless tasks? Certainly they had their daily lives to live. But there were those who kept watching.

Mary and Joseph certainly had expectations of a Messiah, even if they weren't expecting to be so closely involved in His arrival. The shepherds watching their sheep knew about their coming Savior when the angel interrupted their night. Why else would they have been so excited to run to the stable? Anna and Simeon kept their vigil in the temple and lived to see the Child. My favorite watchers, however, were the magi, who trusted God's sign and started their long journey of faith.

—w—

I too know what's coming. That's because He's already here. But I still watch once more in amazement to relive the arrival. To feel His presence. To welcome His grace and love and gift of life.

"I wait for the Lord more than watchmen wait for the morning, more than watchmen wait for the morning" (Ps. 130:6).

Like the watchers at a parade who crane their necks and strain their ears for the first sign of the processional, I can hear the band of angels before they even turn the corner. I stare down the street, looking, hoping, focusing. I once again hear the music, the carols.

I join Mary and Joseph in welcoming His coming. Like the shepherds, I put aside my mindless tasks and run to the stable. Once more I follow the star on my own faith journey.

O Dear Jesus! May I not be the casual observer, but the watcher who yearns to follow Your example. The watcher who expects only the best from my Lord... His forgiveness, His love, His peace, His joy!

This Can't Wait!
(A Christmas Conversation)

The tiny baby was lifted from her mother's womb. She weighed just a little more than a pound. If they had waited any longer, her mom would have died. The baby's alarming vital signs raced across the monitor screen. One nurse rushed forward to take her away but another held up her hand.

"Let the pastor baptize her first."

With the application of water and words, a calmness came over the little girl. And the pediatric nurse began to work the medical miracles that would save her life.

—w—

Some things can't wait. There is an urgency to emergencies. A waiting room in an emergency room seems like a contradiction in terms. If it truly *is* an emergency, it *can't* wait. Sometimes the most important person in a medical emergency is the person who triages... who determines who can and cannot wait. And also who is beyond hope.

There are other non-life-threatening-but-still-important things that can't wait. I remember a flight when my daughter, two years old at the time, absolutely *had* to use the bathroom just when our plane was taking off. I can still see myself struggling up the inclined aisle towards the front of the cabin. I guess the flight attendant didn't want an accident on the seat either, or she would never have let me out of my seatbelt.

Emergencies and bathroom visits seem to go hand in hand. Snow pants and boots used to stand between me and the bathroom when I was the little girl who had kept playing in the snow past her limit. Carrie Anne used to tell her younger brothers to just "do a little dance" if they found themselves in trouble. As adults, with or without children, convenient bathroom facilities are key to an enjoyable outing.

Sometimes we use the phrase, "I can't wait." Now while this can be an emergency situation, more often it is an expression of impatience. I can't wait for my children to come home. I can't wait for my birthday. I can't wait to open my presents. I can't wait for Christmas.

When we lived in Arkansas and our children were still quite young, the last Christmas Eve service didn't end until way past their bedtime. Of course we couldn't open gifts without Daddy! Christmas morning was another church service, and their dad was up earlier than they were, off to prepare for worship. The people at church that morning asked our children what they had received for Christmas. I was on the receiving end of some pretty strange looks when they said they hadn't opened their gifts yet. It was almost noon before we finally got around to unwrapping them. That's just the way it was. "I can't wait" wasn't even an issue. Of course you can wait. Because you *are* waiting!

—ᴍ—

"This can't wait" was certainly on God's mind when He promised a Messiah to a disobedient Adam and Eve. Immediately their salvation needed to be secured with the hope of His saving power. Believing in God's promise kept that hope and salvation alive during the long wait for fulfillment.

But once that fulfillment was set in motion, there was a sense of urgency. Pregnancies do that. There is no turning back. The final weeks came and the unavoidable trip to Bethlehem was pressed on them by the Romans. No regular shelter available meant the next closest thing would have to do. There was no stopping this birth. The angels came that very night to shepherds who then couldn't wait to rush to the stable.

Leaving My Guilt at the Cross

Finally there was a lull for the Holy Family, but not for long. The arrival of the magi set another emergency in motion. Bethlehem was just a short day's trip from Jerusalem, and Herod's men would soon be on their way to kill the child. Joseph believed the angel's warning that he couldn't wait. Off they hurried that night to flee the sword of death.

God knows when we are just impatient and also when we really can't wait. He knows and would never hold back when He's really needed. Yet sometimes when our physical life depends on it, He chooses in His wisdom when to intervene with the power only He can bring.

But the time He never says wait is when our eternal life is in jeopardy, when we are beyond hope of ever saving ourselves. This is the gift He knows we need, the one He freely gives... faith in the saving power of that small child who became the sacrifice for what we couldn't pay.

And I don't have to wait. He's given me the gift and also opened it for me. He couldn't wait for me to open it because I didn't have it within me to do it. He opened the gift of life for me... to me. It clothes me, surrounds me, fills me.

It couldn't wait because I was that special... *and* that important.

The Gift of Giving
(A Christmas Conversation)

"What's this for?"

I had just given a gift to a good friend of mine to thank her for something special she had done for me. It was the next day and now she was handing *me* a gift.

"Oh, I just *had* to give you something in return for your gift."

She couldn't help it. She couldn't let me be the last one. I quickly realized that if I didn't break this up, I could be headed into a never-ending cycle of gifting with someone who had the "gift of giving."

—⁂—

Christmas is the giving time of year. It's a good thing to give.

There was a study done recently about giving. Two groups of people were given $100 each to spend. One group was told to spend it all on themselves, while the other group had to spend it on others. The results of the follow-up interviews showed that those who gave to others were much happier than those who had given to themselves. Our Lord tells us it is more blessed to give than to receive, and now social science has proved it!

—⁂—

The Scriptures are full of stories of giving, including when, how, and what to give. Give when someone asks you for something. Don't hold back if it's possible to help out someone. We are reminded that when we do give generously it will come back to us. "A good measure, pressed down, shaken together and running over, will be poured into our laps" (Luke 6:38). If only I would always trust those words!

We are also told to give quietly, not publicly or for public adulation and credit. The left hand should never know what the right hand is doing, according to God. That sounds like I need to have a split personality. But really it's saying that giving should be my way of life, a natural outpouring, not a conscious effort on my part.

The greatest giver is our Lord. I can't keep up with His gift giving, but that doesn't mean I should just take it in stride, not even acknowledging His generosity. As a good Lutheran I was raised to give Him my "time, talents, and treasures." I know I also need to give back to Him my praise, my thanks, the glory.

But there is something more that I can give to God... something that He really wants. It's my heart.

Now there are many meanings for "heart": Emotion... enthusiasm... passion... love and affection. It's my innermost character and feelings... my core... the vital part of who I am. This is the part of me that I can't hide from Him, the part that needs His constant cleansing and renewing so that it is willing and ready to be used... by Him.

This gift to Him costs nothing. And yet it costs everything when I realize what I need to give up in order to give my heart to my Lord. It isn't a one-time gift. I wish it could be. But I know when I sometimes hold back... when He doesn't have all of me.

When I think about the "treasure" I give to my family at Christmas, I'm so excited to see their reaction opening their gifts. I'm more excited for them to get my gift than I am for myself when I open my own presents!

When I think about the "treasure" I can give to my Lord, knowing He gave me the greatest gift of all, I know He and I both feel this excitement and joy of giving too.

And I can feel His warm embrace, accepting me and what I offer Him.

Leaving My Guilt at the Cross

I can only hope to show Him my appreciation by continuing to give generously to others and also continuing to give to Him... my time, my life, my heart.

It's a wonderful circle... one that I don't want to break.

What Did You Expect?
(A Christmas and New Year Conversation)

There were no billboards along the dark highway that late night in northern Alabama. We finally saw the lights of a Holiday Inn and were sure we had found a place for us and our two little ones. But the price was so steep we had to move on. Finally we stopped at another well-known motel chain, this one with good rates. We opened the door to our room... and were greeted by two sagging beds and the promised crib that I was sure one good bounce would shake apart. The giant crack in the toilet seat was an added feature to this disaster. But it was reasonably clean and we had no other choice. Well what do you expect when you don't make a reservation and you wait too long to stop? Cuddling my baby in the depression... the bed's and mine... I fell asleep staring at the bare light bulb dangling from the ceiling in the center of the room.

It's really wonderful when our expectations are exceeded. Whatever we were hoping for turns into the greatest day, the greatest experience, the greatest place ever. We just bask in the wonder of it all!

But when our expectations aren't met... when we're disappointed in the promises we have read about that don't materialize, when people don't live up to our hopes, when our faith is shattered... what do we do? What *can* we do? Certainly we can walk away and learn from our misplaced dreams. Sometimes that isn't an option, however, so we just make the best of it and hope for a change in the path we're on.

There are other times when creativity can help. When we were traveling through Michigan in the early 80's we stopped at a rest area along the interstate. Three-year-old Carrie Anne clung to me in terror when she saw the hole in the ground that we were expected to use in place of a regular toilet. I turned the whole thing into an adventure by suggesting we pretend we were like Laura on the TV show *Little House on the Prairie*. Luckily she trusted me to hold her and bought into the whole scenario. (Perhaps this was a preparation for her later adventures in Peace Corps!)

There is no way Mary was expecting to deliver her first-born child in a stable. After all, this was God's Son. What could He be thinking of to drop her into this location? Hadn't He prepared for this? It wasn't like He didn't have time or didn't know what was going to happen. Oh that's right. He *did* know what was going to happen. There would be humble visitors who would feel welcome and right at home in these surroundings.

There were shepherds in the fields... the first to hear about the birth. Obviously they knew about the promised Messiah, since the angels didn't spend a lot of time explaining the message. "For unto you is born this day in the city of David a Saviour, which is Christ the Lord" (Luke 2:11 KJV). They knew the Messiah would be a descendent of David, perhaps just like they were. They knew that the Christ was the Messiah and was God.

And they may have had other expectations as to what the Messiah would be like. Perhaps another king and warrior like David. Perhaps the rescuer from the Romans. Perhaps the Divine Conqueror of poverty and unwanted circumstances.

But the "glory of the Lord shone round about them" (Luke 2:9 KJV) and changed everything.

Leaving My Guilt at the Cross

Certainly the baby they gazed upon in the manger wasn't even close to what they had imagined in their minds and hearts. Yet they believed. They didn't walk away and they didn't "make the best of it" because He wasn't exactly what they were expecting. And they didn't need to create something greater than what was there. They believed not what their senses were telling them, not what the world would dismiss as too incredible to be true. They believed the message from the angels immediately, without discussion. That was a transforming night for them.

I have expectations for each new year. I expect things from myself... things I want to accomplish... things I want to change. I have expectations from others too, and I'm sure at times I'll have to "make the best of it" or create an adventure to get me through.

I don't have the expectation, however, that I won't live through another year. I do have plans, you know. But if it isn't meant to be, that worst-case scenario is really the *best*-case scenario.

I didn't make a reservation, but He's made one for me. I know there are still friends and family who don't understand His promise, His saving grace. But I know that it's never too late for them to answer His call because the same vacancy sign is there for everyone.

The place He's prepared for me is beyond my greatest expectations. And the best thing is... I don't have to worry about the room rate. It's already paid for with His gift certificate!

You will go out in joy and be led forth in peace." Isaiah 55:12

Afterword

The conversation continues....

"If you don't feel close to God, guess who moved?" It seems I'm doing that dance more often than I care to admit. Of course I want to take credit when I feel connected to God, and I want to blame Him when I don't.

I know I can never really do enough, say enough, try hard enough in order to feel close to Him... to *stay* close to Him. So I let it go and remind myself once more of His forgiving grace. I drop my guilt and enjoy the times when I'm hand in hand with my Lord. And I reflect on the emptiness when I'm not feeling that connection.

He's right there even when I'm not paying attention. And when I realize I've once again been ignoring Him, I hear His voice calling me... and it is constantly doing just that... and I resume my chat with my Savior... truly listening to my Lord.

And once again I'm showered with His love... overwhelmed by the joy... His joy!

Leaving my guilt at the cross,

Christine

About the Author:

T eacher, musician, pastor's wife, mother of three adult children, and a mature but still growing Christian are all part of my identity.

I grew up in a small city in northern Michigan and now reside in a much larger city in southern California. As a pastor's family we enjoyed the love of three congregations in Tennessee, Arkansas, and California for over thirty-five years.

For many years I taught at various schools and at all levels from kindergarten to college. During that time I also earned my Masters in Education and served as Director of Music at our California church. All of this abundance of experiences, insights, and memories inspire my writing, my speaking, and my walk with my Lord.

Writing and speaking about the joy of being God's child has always been part of my life, but more recently I have taken it to the professional level. My weekly inspirational blogs are read worldwide and are the basis of this book. I have also written and produced three plays about people and events in the Gospels that give fresh insight into those times. My speaking engagements in the southern California area have reached several hundred women on the topics of Peace, Time, Power and Strength, and, of course, Joy!

Made in the USA
San Bernardino, CA
28 March 2019